CAPILANO COLLEGE LIBRARY

PQ2012C66Y92

MONTESQUIEU REVISITED

D0409239

CONROY PETER V

WITHDRAWN

Montesquieu Revisited

Twayne's World Authors Series
French Literature

David O'Connell, Editor
Georgia State University

TWAS 829

MONTESQUIEU
Courtesy of the Bibliothèque Nationale

Montesquieu Revisited

Peter V. Conroy, Jr.

University of Illinois, Chicago

Twayne Publishers • New York
Maxwell Macmillan Canada • Toronto
Maxwell Macmillan International • New York   Oxford   Singapore   Sydney

Montesquieu Revisited
Peter V. Conroy, Jr.

Copyright © 1992 by Twayne Publishers

All rights reserved. No part of this book may be reproduced or transmitted in any form or by any means, electronic or mechanical, including photocopying, recording, or by any information storage and retrieval system, without permission in writing from the Publisher.

Twayne Publishers
Macmillan Publishing Company
866 Third Avenue
New York, New York 10022

Maxwell Macmillan Canada, Inc.
1200 Eglinton Avenue East
Suite 200
Don Mills, Ontario M3C 3N1

Macmillan Publishing Company is part of the Maxwell Communication Group of Companies.

Library of Congress Cataloging-in-Publication Data

Conroy, Peter V.
    Montesquieu revisited / Peter V. Conroy, Jr.
        p.   cm. — (Twayne's world author series ; TWAS 829. French literature)
    Includes bibliographical references and index.
    ISBN 0-8057-8273-7
    1. Montesquieu, Charles de Secondat, baron de, 1689-1755
—Criticism and interpretation.   I. Title.   II. Series: Twayne's world authors series ; TWAS 829.   III. Series: Twayne's world authors series.   French literature.
PQ2012.C66   1992
848'.509—dc20   92-18575
                                                                 CIP

The paper used in this publication meets the minimum requirements of American National Standard for Information Sciences—Permanence of Paper for Printed Library Materials. ANSI Z3948-1984. ∞™

10 9 8 7 6 5 4 3 2 1

Printed in the United States of America

Contents

Preface

In 1968 J. Robert Loy published in Twayne's World Authors Series a *Montesquieu* that was an excellent introduction to the writer as he was then understood. Most of Loy's attention was devoted to an analysis of *The Spirit of the Laws*; discussion of Montesquieu's many other writings was crowded into the remaining half of his volume. Montesquieu was presented as a man of one book, a masterpiece to be sure, but one that fixed him seemingly forever in our minds.

This volume is entitled *Montesquieu Revisited* because, although Montesquieu has been much studied in the past, he is currently enjoying a major critical reevaluation. The intellectual and literary climate in eighteenth-century studies has changed radically in the last three decades and Montesquieu is one of the figures who has been most affected by this revolution in scholarship.

Despite his unchallenged status as a classic, Montesquieu has always been a problematic figure. In the more than 200 years since his death the président (a title referring to Montesquieu's position as magistrate, which he retained all his life) has enjoyed enormous prestige and influence. In academe he has long been recognized as a seminal thinker whose pioneering work in the social sciences was critical to their very existence. In the practical world his influence as a political theorist left an indelible impression on our own Founding Fathers and the Framers of the American Constitution.

Nonetheless, such an outstanding success masked a contradictory reality. Though much referred to, Montesquieu was actually being read less and less by the middle of the twentieth century, especially in those disciplines that he adumbrated. What he had done as a pathbreaker was largely surpassed by others who pushed the field far beyond his original scope. Ironically, then, Montesquieu, abandoned by the social sciences to which he had given birth, retained his readers in literature where he had never been much at home. As Loy's book illustrates, Montesquieu was really a figure on the margins of literary study. In classes offered as literature, he was read as a *philosophe* for his "ideas," for his discussion of politics and government, for his role in the intellectual ferment known as the Enlightenment. Admitting Montesquieu into literature classes was justified by his importance in the literary history of the eighteenth century, an age in which literature was tightly bound to the history of ideas. But, while his style was often admired, he was never considered a "creative" author like the poets, playwrights, or novelists of his time.

In the past 20 or 30 years, however, that situation has changed dramatically. No longer is Montesquieu considered almost exclusively as the author of *The Spirit of the Laws* and a spokesman for the Age of Ideas. Today he is also recognized as a novelist and *The Persian Letters* has finally taken its rightful place as one of the major novels of the eighteenth century. *Montesquieu Revisited* belongs, as its title clearly suggests, to this wave of reevaluation. Not only do I recapitulate the traditional interpretations of Montesquieu the Enlightenment thinker but I also present the "new" novelist. Almost as many of my pages here are devoted to *The Persian Letters* as to the *Laws*. Moreover, besides analyzing the political theorist and the novelist, I examine the historian, the tourist and travel writer, the amateur scientist, and the social scribbler of oriental tales in the fashion of his times. Providing a complete picture of the author and reflecting traditional as well as recent scholarship, *Montesquieu Revisited* is intended for those who, reading Montesquieu for the first time, need an up-to-date synthesis of his work and ideas; for more advanced undergraduates who want an orientation that can serve as a stimulus for additional reading and research; and, finally, for graduate students who are looking for interpretations that will challenge them to reconsider Montesquieu from more daring and provocative perspectives.

My study places Montesquieu squarely within his eighteenth-century context and, simultaneously, shows how he belongs to our own time. These two tasks are difficult to reconcile since the two periods are indeed different. But a *classic* is precisely one who belongs intimately to the time in which he or she wrote and to the time in which he or she is read. Whether I have accomplished that task will be for my readers to judge.

The method used throughout this book is straightforward and has two main components. First, I offer an overview of each work, a sort of organizational table or structural analysis that reveals the distinct parts of the work as well as how they make a whole. This overview takes several forms. It consists of an analytic and descriptive outline for *The Spirit of the Laws* and the *Considerations on the Causes of the Greatness of the Romans and their Decadence*; plot and thematic articulation for *The Persian Letters*; itinerary and calendar for the notebooks of his voyages in

Europe. With *Mes Pensées* (My thoughts) and the minor works, I seek out organizational patterns through a series of categories that address the principal issues separately and that indicate the coherence of the whole when taken together. Explaining the overall rhetorical structure and organization of each work provides a first interpretation since that critical gesture defines the main lines of argumentation and the principal articulations and interrelationships of the material within. The overview is followed by a close reading of the individual parts. Not all issues can be discussed, especially in a work as long and as complex as the *Laws*. I have had to make choices, but I have always tried to make them with the shape and meaning of the whole in mind. By focusing alternately on large and small, on structure and detail, I try to provide a critical framework that reveals the total significance of each work while it interprets the key parts that flesh out that whole. Keeping these orientations in mind, my readers will be able to investigate on their own what I have not been able to cover. *Montesquieu Revisited* is in no way intended as a last word or definitive comment. On the contrary, it is meant as an inspiration to subsequent reading, an indication that many other possible interpretations do exist, and an invitation to show readers how they can approach Montesquieu by themselves.

Chronology

1689 Charles-Louis de Secondat born 18 January at the chateau of La Brède near Bordeaux, the second child and the first son of Jacques de Secondat and Marie-Françoise de Pesnel.

1700 On 11 August enters the Collège of the Oratorians in Juilly, near Paris.

1705 Returns to Bordeaux to continue his studies at the University of Bordeaux and to begin his law career.

1708 After receiving his degree as a *bachelier* (29 July) and then as *licencié* (12 August), he is admitted to the bar as an *avocat au Parlement* on 14 August. Although he is officially still the baron de la Brède, he begins to use his uncle's name, Montesquieu.

1709–1713 Further studies in Paris, probably as a law clerk.

1714 After the death of his father in 1713 (his mother died in 1696), becomes a *conseiller* to the Bordeaux Parlement.

1715 Marries Jeanne Lartigue.

1716 His uncle, Jean-Baptiste, dies (24 April) and his son, Jean-Baptiste, is born (10 February). Montesquieu takes over his uncle's office and becomes *président à mortier*. Now he officially assumes the name Montesquieu. Elected a member of the Académie de Bordeaux.

1721 *Les Lettres persanes* published anonymously: its great success leads to many imitations and to a quick second edition.

1724 Introduced into Mme de Lambert's salon, a famous literary circle.

1725 *Temple de Gnide* published anonymously.

1726 Sells his legal office of *président* in Bordeaux and in effect retires from active legal life.

1727	Elected member of Académie Françoise on 20 December and received into its ranks on 24 January 1728.
April 1728–May 1731	Travels in Europe: his itinerary includes Vienna, Hungary, Italy, Austria, Germany, and England.
July 1734	*Les Considérations sur les causes de la grandeur des Romains et de leur décadence* published in Holland. A success in England, it receives mixed reviews at best in France.
1735	Begins work in earnest on *De l'Esprit des lois* which will fill the rest of his life. Some chapters date back to earlier writings, but the total scheme and organization come into focus as he writes.
1738	Marriage of his daughter Thérèse.
1740	Marriage of his son, Jean-Baptiste.
1742	*Arsace et Isménie.*
1745	Marriage of his favorite child, Denise, to a cousin, Godefroy de Secondat.
1748	In October *De l'Esprit des lois* is finally published by Barrillot in Geneva, again without the author's name. But the book has been at the printer's for a year and Montesquieu is known as its author.
1750	"Défense de *l'Esprit des Lois.*" His masterpiece provokes controversy and spawns a quarrel in which Montesquieu has to defend himself and his intentions.
1752	*De l'Esprit des lois* is placed on the Catholic church's Index of Forbidden Books in Rome.
1753	Elected director of the Académie Française on 2 April. Is asked to write the article "Goût" which will appear in the *Encyclopédie* posthumously in 1757.
1754	A new edition of the *Lettres persanes* published by Pierre Marteau at Cologne. In the preface Montesquieu first mentions "the secret chain."
1755	Montesquieu dies in Paris on 10 February after having fallen ill on 29 January during a brief trip to the capital. He is buried the following day at Saint Sulpice. Only Diderot from the *philosophes* attends the funeral.

1757   Second edition of *De l'Esprit* finished by Richer working
from the author's notes.

Chapter One

Biography of Montesquieu

Charles-Louis de Secondat, baron de la Brède and de Montesquieu, président of the Bordeaux Parlement, was born in the chateau of La Brède, just outside Bordeaux, on 18 January 1689 into an established aristocratic family that included both *noblesse d'épée* (soldiers) and *noblesse de robe* (magistrates).

The Secondat family had military connections that dated back to the Protestant Henry of Navarre. After he became king of France under the name Henri IV, that monarch rewarded his loyal soldier Jacques II de Secondat by raising his property of Montesquieu to a barony in 1606. Jacques's son, Jean-Baptiste-Gaston, married into a family of magistrates and became a *président à mortier* (the presiding judge on an appeals court) in the Bordeaux Parlement. The latter's eldest son, Jean-Baptiste, succeeded him in this office. Another son, Jacques III de Secondat, was the father of our Montesquieu.

In 1686 this Jacques de Secondat married Marie-Françoise de Pesnel whose dowry included the barony of La Brède and its chateau. This property and title passed to her son when she died in October 1696 during childbirth. Jacques and Marie-Françoise had six children, of which four survived. Our Montesquieu was the second child and the eldest son. Both of his sisters became nuns and his younger brother a priest. At his baptism, a beggar served as his godfather so that, despite his wealth and social position, he would never forget that the poor were his brothers. His early years were spent at La Brède where he grew up with the peasants and acquired the heavy local accent that he would never lose despite his travels abroad and his sojourns in Paris.

At the age of 11, Charles-Louis was sent to the *collège* at Juilly, not far from Paris. By the early eighteenth century, the Jesuits had established a near monopoly on education in France. Staffed by the Congregation of the Oratory, Juilly was a successful alternative to their pedagogical domination. It had a fine reputation, attracting students from great distances. That it was also progressive in its thinking might explain why it was criticized by some in power for being too liberal and independent. The most celebrated Oratorian of this time was the philosopher Malebranche. His philosophy inspired Juilly even though it is doubtful that he visited the school much or that Montesquieu ever met him. Although by eighteenth-century standards innovative in its attention to French and history, the Juilly curriculum still focused on Latin and the Latin authors.

His studies at Juilly finished, Montesquieu returned to Bordeaux in September 1705. There he began his study of law. Within a few years he earned his degree and became a lawyer associated with the parlement. At some point in this period Charles-Louis began to use his uncle's name, Montesquieu. This uncle, Jean-Baptiste, was his father's older brother and thus first in line to inherit the Secondat name and property. He had no surviving children, however, and had decided that, upon his death, his nephew would inherit his name, his property, and his office as *président à mortier* in the Bordeaux Parlement.

From 1709 to 1713 Montesquieu was in Paris continuing his legal studies, probably as a law clerk in the office of some acquaintance of his uncle's. He also began to make the first contacts with the literary and scientific circles that he would later frequent whenever he was in the capital. These years provided him with experiences as well as with sights and sounds he would later record in *Les Lettres persanes* (*The Persian Letters*). Although there is little documentation for this period of Montesquieu's life, we do know that he found a mentor in the Oratorian priest Pierre-Nicolas Desmolets. Curious about things scientific, an interest which would remain with him all his life, Montesquieu attended meetings, both public and private, of various learned societies. He renewed his friendship with a schoolmate from Juilly, Nicolas Fréret, a traveler and specialist on China, something quite rare at the time. Through Fréret, he also met a real Chinese named Hoange.[1] Foreign travel and different cultures were therefore introduced to Montesquieu at this formative period.

Changes in his life now came fast. His father, Jacques de Secondat, died on 15 November 1713 and Montesquieu returned home. Suddenly he was the lord of the manor of La Brède, responsible for a sizable piece of property and holding all the feudal rights and obligations over it. Although debts remained, some extending back to his mother's dowry, the fortune bequeathed to him was considerable and the properties extensive. Montesquieu endeavored all his life to augment the inheritance that he would pass on in his turn. By all accounts he did so successfully.

In March 1715 he signed a marriage contract and the next month married Jeanne Lartigue. There was little romance in their relationship, it seems. Nonetheless, she became an effective manager of the estate and thereby allowed Montesquieu the time and freedom for his travels and his studies. She bore him three children, the last of whom, Denise, helped her father as a secretary and research assistant when he was working on *De l'Esprit des lois* (*The Spirit of the Laws*). Jeanne was a Protestant who never gave up her faith to embrace the Catholicism of her husband. Surely part of Montesquieu's well-known tolerance stems from his personal experience both with his wife's and his own ancestor's Protestantism. Her religion never interfered with her duties as wife, helpmate, and mother, and Montesquieu must have noticed that holding divergent religious beliefs did not preclude their deeper compatibility.

Shortly after Montesquieu's marriage, his uncle, Jean-Baptiste de Secondat, died (24 April 1716), leaving him his title, his property, and his office. Now he could officially call himself baron de Montesquieu as well as baron de La Brède. In addition, he became a *président à mortier* of the Bordeaux Parlement. With his uncle's inheritance, he repaid several outstanding debts and was able to start putting his entire estate on a firmer financial footing.

During this same period Montesquieu became a member of the recently founded Academy of Bordeaux. The center of intellectual and social life in the provincial capital, the academy had been incorporated by royal decree only in 1713 along the lines of academies in Paris and other cities. Here he was able to satisfy that taste for science he had acquired at Juilly. He read a few papers, some of which have been lost; and the main value of those that survive is to indicate the future directions of his interests.

Probably in 1717 Montesquieu began working on *The Persian Letters*. Four years later he brought the manuscript with him to Paris and showed it to his mentor Desmolets who predicted it would be a bestseller: "that will sell like hotcakes," he is supposed to have said.[2] A French-Protestant publisher in Amsterdam named Desbordes printed the novel in the spring or early summer of 1721. It was an immediate success. Although published anonymously, a frequent practice whenever an author was unsure about how his work would be received, it was quickly attributed to Montesquieu who waited years before acknowledging that he had indeed written it. He became nonetheless the darling of the exclusive Parisian social milieu that he had only glimpsed years before as a student.

At first he tended toward the more libertine sections of the upper classes. He appeared at festivities given by Mme de Prie, the mistress of the prime minister, the duc de Bourbon, at her estate of Belébat. He also frequented Chantilly where Mlle de Clermont, the sister of the duc de Bourbon, hosted her friends. While there is no conclusive proof, some critics have suggested that Montesquieu was not just an observer of this "life in the fast lane." Some evidence points to a passionate if momentary attachment to the marquise de Grave. Supposedly he described the love affair of Mlle de Clermont and the duc de Melun in "Le Temple de Gnide" (Temple of Gnidus) in 1725, an erotic novel disguised as a translation from the Greek. Rumor also suggested an amatory liaison between Montesquieu and Mlle de Clermont, which the "Temple" is also said to recount in its vague fashion.

But frivolity was not all that he discovered in Paris. He also made contact with the more serious domains of politics and literature. In the realm of politics, the most important circle he frequented was known as the "Club de l'Entresol" because it met on Saturdays in the *entresol*, a sort of mezzanine between the ground and the first floors, in the home of the Président Hénault on the Place Vendôme. Discussions turned on economics and politics. The club attracted a distinguished group of diplomats, magistrates, and men of letters, both Frenchmen and foreigners visiting the capital. Montesquieu's contribution to this intellectual ferment was his "Dialogue de Sylla et d'Eucrate" (Dialogue of Sylla and Eucrates), which he might have begun in 1724 but did not present to the club until 1727. It was reportedly not received with much enthusiasm. Although the Entresol had a reputation for liberal thinking and thus was somewhat feared by the prime minister, Montesquieu's participation did him little harm in the eyes of society.

For matters literary, he was introduced into the salon of Mme de Lambert. In keeping with a French tradition that went back to Mme de Rambouillet and her "Blue Room," Mme de Lambert held an open house one day a week, Tuesdays, when she received friends, acquaintances, and the social elite in her *hôtel* (the eighteenth-century term for an elaborate town house). Her salon attracted the leading writers of the day, including Fontenelle, Marivaux, Crébillon, and Houdar de la Motte. All manner of literary questions were discussed and often authors brought their latest production to read aloud. This reading served both to publicize the new work among those influential individuals who could have some impact on the larger public's reaction, and to allow that same inner circle the opportunity to comment upon and criticize the work presented, and thus to help fashion the final product.

From 1721 until 1728 Montesquieu made numerous trips to Paris and lived there for extended periods. The lure of Paris meant that he did not attend to his legal duties in Bordeaux. It also indicates that he did not demonstrate much interest in his wife and two young children. He returned to Bordeaux for a short period in 1726 in order to conclude the negotiations for the sale of his office as *président à mortier*. In effect, Montesquieu retired from his career as a magistrate at age 37. He claimed to understand the law, but to have no real comprehension of how it worked or of its processes. Through this sale he was able both to raise the money needed to finance his continued residence in Paris and later to travel through Europe. He did not, however, completely abandon the three-generation-old family tradition of being a *président* because he stipulated in the contract that his son could repurchase the office when he came of age.

Back in Paris he continued to frequent the salon of Mme de Lambert and the Club de l'Entresol. Probably with the latter in mind he composed his "Considérations sur les richesses d'Espagne" ("Considerations on the Wealth of Spain"), while Mme de Lambert, true to her role as *salonnière* and muse of literature, began her campaign to get Montesquieu elected to the Académie Française. Election to that august body had always been (and still is) based on public recognition of a significant body of work *and* a careful cultivation of those individuals who actually cast the votes. The latter activity was ideally suited to the nature and scope of a salon. Despite such powerful support, Montesquieu faced a number of obstacles. He frequented less-than-reputable circles, including the politically dangerous Entresol and the débauchés around Mme de Prie and Mlle de Clermont. His published works included the erotic "Temple de Gnide" and the even more provocative *Persian Letters*. According to Montesquieu's son, the candidate himself went to see the prime minister, Cardinal Fleury, who opposed his election. Fleury's primary objection was to *The Persian Letters*, "which he had never read . . . but which he knew well enough thanks to an extremely faithful abstract which someone had given him and which made the hair on his head stand up."[3] Always the lawyer, Montesquieu replied that he did not admit being the author but he would not deny it either, and that furthermore he preferred to give up a seat in the Académie rather than give up the title of author. He also challenged Fleury to read the whole book himself, rather than relying on a tendentious abstract. The cardinal read the book, liked it, and withdrew his opposition. Montesquieu was elected to the Académie Française on 20 December 1727, and officially installed on 24 January 1728. He delivered the required acceptance speech, a dull and routine *éloge* (praise) of Louis de Sacy, the academician whom he replaced.

In the spring of 1728, after having attended only a few meetings of the Académie, Montesquieu left Paris for an extensive trip through Europe. Distances were long, the means of transportation slow in the eighteenth century: the trip lasted three years. From April 1728 to May 1731, Montesquieu gathered facts and recorded his observations about the cultures and the countries he visited. The most valuable result of the whole voyage was his contact with England. There he saw in practice a democracy that combined religious freedom and mercantile activity. He also observed firsthand the British parliamentary system that he would later discuss in *The Spirit of the Laws*.

The first leg of the journey took Montesquieu and his traveling companion, Count Waldegrave, to Vienna where he met Prince Eugene, the great general who with Marlborough had defeated the French under Villars at Malplacquet and later saved Vienna from the Turks. From there he visited salt mines in Hungary. He passed through what is today southern Austria on his way to Venice, arriving there in August. After visiting a number of northern Italian cities, he reached Rome on 19 January 1729. The French presence in Rome was considerable thanks to its diplomatic corps at the Vatican. He listened to stories and gossip, opinions and prejudices. He felt for the first time the power of art directly when he saw the masterpieces of Raphael, Michelangelo, and da Vinci. He visited the sites of Roman history that he knew so well from his reading. In the summer he traveled north, through the Brenner Pass to Innsbruck and up through Germany to Amsterdam where he boarded a boat bound for England.

He arrived in London on 3 November 1729. His English friends Count Waldegrave and Lord Chesterfield introduced him into the most prestigious intellectual and social circles. He was named a fellow of the Royal Society in February 1730 and joined the Freemasons in May of the same year, as Voltaire would later do during his exile in England. He attended several sessions of Parliament. His written accounts, while short, show that he was able to follow the debate quite well. He was admitted to court and recorded several of his conversations with Queen Caroline.

His grand tour over, Montesquieu returned home in May 1731. For two years he worked at La Brède, classifying his notes and laying out a new garden. Doubtless in England he had seen the new style of landscape garden, which was designed to appear natural, and had decided to replace his French garden and its characteristically geometric alley-ways and symmetrical design. When he left La Brède for Paris in the spring of 1733, he had with him a manuscript of the *Les Considérations sur les causes de la grandeur des Romains et de leur décadence* (*Considerations on the Causes of the Greatness of the Romans and their Decadence*). This was a serious historical work, based on extensive reading in Latin sources, and therefore very unlike his previous publications. The book was published in Holland after being read in proof and corrected by Montesquieu's longtime friend and the tutor of his son, the Jesuit Père Castel.

For the next fifteen years Montesquieu worked patiently and dili-gently at his masterpiece, *De l'Esprit des lois* (literally *On the Spirit of Laws,* but usually translated as *The Spirit of the Laws*). This immense book pulled together the work of a lifetime. He reworked thoughts he had expressed in *The Persian Letters*; he inserted essays he had written earlier like the "Considerations on the Wealth of Spain" and which were simply waiting their proper context; he called upon what he had learned in conversations and by experience during his grand tour through Europe and his many visits to Paris. The goal he set himself was not a traditional one. Daring and innovative, he was searching for the mecha-nisms that explain how laws work, why they are different from country to country and culture to culture, and how they nonetheless conform to certain basic principles.

To accomplish this great work, Montesquieu amassed a fine library that was rich in historical and legal authors. The room where he worked and the volumes he consulted can still be seen at the chateau of La Brède by any curious tourist. He devoted himself to this work even to the point of nearly going blind: his severe myopia and ophthalmia worsened due to his extensive reading. Eventually his failing eyesight forced him to use a number of secretaries and copyists to read and write for him. In the midst of his daunting scholarly undertaking, Montesquieu still found time for other activities. He remained an active lord of the manor, taking a close interest in his property and in the peasants who worked it. Fair in all his dealings, he was not therefore any less exacting about what was due him. His property was always a productive one. Perhaps the commercial nature of his fortune (he produced a good-qual-ity wine that he sold principally in England) explains why he linked economics and politics in his work. Finally, he arranged marriages for his three children and thus assured the continuity of his family name and the fortune he considered it his duty to maintain.

He did not remain at La Brède for any extended period of time except for a span of three years between September 1743 and September 1746 when he married off his daughter Denise and probably completed a first draft of the *Laws*. He traveled frequently to Paris and reappeared in those aristocratic circles and salons that he so much enjoyed. His good friend Mme de Lambert having died in 1733, he now frequented the salons of Mme de Tencin, Mme du Deffand, and Mme Geoffrin, among others. Here he would regularly meet many of the other outstanding literary figures of the time: Diderot, d'Alembert, Buffon, Marivaux, Duclos, Fontenelle, Crébillon. On occasion he even composed a few works in a frivolous and mildly erotic style, for example, *Arsace et Isménie* (1742) and *Céphise et l'Amour* (Cephise and Cupid, 1743).

In late October 1748 *The Spirit of the Laws* was published in Geneva by Barrillot. Montesquieu's friends immediately greeted the new work with enthusiasm. By the end of 1749 about 22 other editions, including translations, had reached all parts of civilized Europe. Some, in their rapid and frequently cursory reading, failed to understand the method or the intention behind the book. Although a long-standing friend of Montesquieu's, Mme du Deffand summed up her reaction with a pun on the title that was made famous by Voltaire's retelling: the book did not contain the spirit of the laws but rather some spirit (i.e., wit) about laws. Misunderstanding gave way to real controversy, however, and soon thereafter a full-scale quarrel that would last until 1752 was being waged in print.

French public reaction was at first muted but then changed to hostile. Jesuits and Jansenists both attacked the *Laws,* in large part because they discerned there a profound indifference to the Christian religion. Montesquieu had given little place to Christianity as a determining force in history, he admired perhaps too much some pagan philosophers, and he discussed moral issues like suicide in nonreligious terms. After keeping silent and allowing others to defend him, Montesquieu finally felt obliged to respond personally to his detractors with his "Défense de *l'Esprit des lois*" (Defense of *The Spirit of the Laws,* 1750). Meanwhile religious authorities in Rome and in Paris were examining the book. From July 1750 until June 1754 the Sorbonne considered censuring it. Five different accusations were drawn up and made public but none was ratified. In Rome, on 29 November 1751, the book was put on the Church's Index, which meant that Catholics were forbidden to read it. At first, the ban was not made public and so the effect of its denunciation was slight. However, several months later, on 2 March

1752, the decree was published and its impact became more substantial.

Despite this official censure, Montesquieu was named director of the Académie Française in 1753. About the same time, D'Alembert asked him to write articles on democracy and despotism for the *Encyclopédie* that he was editing with Diderot. Montesquieu refused, claiming that he had already said all he could on those topics. But he did agree to do something on taste. The "Essai sur le goût" (Essay on taste) would not see its way into print until 1757 and even then it remained unfinished.

December 1754 found Montesquieu once again in Paris. He fell ill on 29 January and his health quickly deteriorated. His sickness held the public's attention. His lodging was filled with friends awaiting developments. Even the king was curious and sent the duc de Nivernais to inquire about his condition. Since Montesquieu had earned an international reputation, he was no common citizen nor was his impending death an everyday matter. On the contrary, his passing was understood as symbolic of the conflict, now approaching its high point, that pitted established religion against the forces of reason and enlightenment. At the foot of his deathbed was waged an ideological battle of which we have a number of somewhat conflicting accounts.

When Montesquieu said that he wanted to make his last confession, an Irish Jesuit named Routh questioned him about the mysteries of the Catholic church and whether he accepted the church's authority. Montesquieu claimed never to have lost his faith and satisfied the confessor about his worthiness to receive the last rites. When the local parish priest arrived, Montesquieu said that he had already made the necessary arrangements with Routh and that he was sure the parish priest would be content with them. Then he made an act of contrition, took communion, and received the church's last rites.

According to Robert Shackleton, there was a bit of partisan sparring before this peaceful ending.[4] The curate wanted to draw the moral lesson for this philosopher suspected of atheism: "Now you are learning, sir, better than anyone else how great God is . . ." But Montesquieu cut him off and finished the phrase: "and how small men are."

A much less pious and edifying version of Montesquieu's final minutes underlines the ideological issues at stake. While the duchesse d'Aiguillon, who was usually present in the sickroom, happened to be absent, Routh slipped in and spoke to Montesquieu alone. The duchesse claimed she overheard Routh badgering the dying man and trying to extort from him some papers, perhaps a corrected manuscript of *The Persian Letters,* or some dramatic deathbed confession that would repudiate his former works. Montesquieu resisted. The papers in question were given to the duchesse who transmitted them to Montesquieu's son.

Montesquieu died on 10 February 1755. The funeral took place in the parish church of Saint-Sulpice where the body was buried. In marked contrast to his illness, which captivated public attention throughout Paris, Montesquieu's actual burial attracted little notice. The only fellow *philosophe* and literary figure who attended the ceremony was Diderot.

Chapter Two

The Persian Letters

This novel was published anonymously in Amsterdam in the spring or early summer of 1721 by Jacques Desbordes. Montesquieu probably began work on it in 1717 and brought the finished manuscript with him to Paris late in 1720 or early in 1721. It was such an enormous and immediate success that over 30 years later Montesquieu himself recounted how the booksellers would pull everyone they met in the street by the sleeve and say, "Monsieur, write me another *Persian Letters*."[1]

Story and Context

As its title itself indicates, *The Persian Letters* is an epistolary novel about several Persians who leave their native land in 1711, travel to Europe, and live in France until 1720. During this whole period they comment upon what they see and experience since it is all so different from what they know in their native Persia. The novel records scenes of social and cultural life in eighteenth-century France and offers short essays on political and philosophical topics. But there is also another plot line. Usbek, the principal character, has left all his wives back in his harem in Ispahan. After enduring his absence for nine years, the harem is rent by dissension and open revolt against the master. The novel ends as Usbek prepares to return to his native land.

This résumé in no way does justice to the importance of this novel or to the impact it had upon its reading public. Immediately upon publication it met with overwhelming success. It was what we would call a runaway best-seller, and this in the days before advertising hype and promotion via the electronic media. Other writers tried to ride Montesquieu's coattails with their own oriental and Persian stories but no subsequent writer ever came close to Montesquieu's effort. His book served to define the "oriental novel" for Europe and the entire century.

Travel and the erotic. Although unexpected, the tremendous success of this novel is in no way unjustified. Montesquieu astutely

11

capitalized on the taste and the interests of his public. He reinvigorated
a traditional theme, that of a visitor discovering a new country, by
reversing the normal pattern and making the visitors new and the
country to be discovered the France that Frenchmen thought they
already knew. He also sprinkled in a bit of spice: Usbek's numerous
wives hidden in their Middle Eastern harem and guarded by an army
of eunuchs was enough to titillate the public and hold their attention
through more intellectually demanding passages about laws and
customs. Before examining the novel's themes in detail, I would
like to look briefly at the wider literary and historical context for
Montesquieu's oriental narrative.

The Persian Letters speaks directly to the early eighteenth-century's
interest in and fascination with travel. Not long before, France and
indeed most of Europe were closed and self-centered communities, ignorant of the world about them. French classical theater, for example,
felt more affinity with the past of Greece and Rome than with the life
of contemporary nations.

Slowly this situation was changing as explorers sailed to the ends of
the earth and brought back tales of their adventures. Chardin visited
Persia, Tavernier Turkey, Bernier and Le Comte China. Jesuit mission-
aries sent back reports, called *relations,* of the lands they visited and the
natives they tried to convert. Those from America are still valuable
historical documents on Indian life as it was lived just as the first
contacts with white men were being made, and the *relations* about China
brought a whole new culture to the attention of Europeans and helped
to make fictional accounts like Montesquieu's more believable. Baron
Lahontan published an account in 1703 of his voyages to America. The
New World, of course, was one of those fabulous places that thrilled
the imagination of Europeans.

As a result of the interest these explorations excited, the time was
ripe for someone to capitalize on the public's fascination with the foreign and the exotic. While not knowing a great deal about foreign
countries or customs, the French had at least been made aware that they
existed. This paradoxical situation of a people interested in what was
foreign because it was foreign and yet at the same time basically incapable of appreciating what was different because it was different, is
succinctly summed up by one of the most famous sentences in the
novel. Rica, one of the Persians, is engaged in conversation with a
Frenchman who finally, almost in desperation, asks "How can you be
Persian?"[2]

Montesquieu, however, does not just ride the crest of this wave of interest in the Near East. He makes the ethnocentric and almost xeno-phobic question quoted above a tool for cultural inquiry by shifting the focus of his novel. Rather than placing a few Frenchmen in a foreign surrounding, the basic situation presented in all the accounts of travels to distant and exotic lands, Montesquieu centers his novel on the Persian visitors who see France as the foreign place, as the alternative to what is right and acceptable in their homeland. This small change in perspective produced an enormous effect. No longer were France and the French the standard used to measure the entire world; now these Persians noticed the follies of French custom and "compared" them to what was right, normal, and correct, that is, to their own practice and prejudice in Persia. In one fell swoop Montesquieu completely turned the world upside down. For his readers, seeing France through a stranger's eyes was at first unusual and amusing; but their vantage point shifted to the critical as flaws became apparent. What had been ac-cepted unquestioningly now was probed from a position outside that automatic consensus. What starts as an innocent variant of tourist lit-erature quickly becomes an uncomfortable questioning of the status quo and a searching inquiry into what is the most logical or intelligent way to behave.

There is one final element of literary history that helps to explain the success of *The Persian Letters*: its licentious and erotic content. Today we are much too blasé and too accustomed to real pornography, either in books or the movies, to appreciate the importance of this factor. While we find this novel full of sociological and anthropological data and informed by a serious study of laws and history, many of its first readers were attracted by the story of the seraglio and Usbek's many wives. This was an age of suggestion and innuendo rather than frank realism and so the reader was prepared to read into the text what the words only implied. Although our modern tastes are not excited by such weak stuff, we must remember that eighteenth-century readers, formed both by the *bienséances* (decorum and reserve) of seventeenth-century classical theater and an underground tradition of allusively erotic writing, were much more impressed. As odd as it may seem to us today, *The Persian Letters* found its way into the *Enfers* (literally, the Hells) of French li-braries, those locked cases that prevented patrons from reading books intentionally kept out of easy circulation. Here, for example, is a pas-sage that simultaneously evokes a voluptuous scene and refuses to give the salacious particulars it promises. Classical French prose is notoriously reticent with concrete details, and here we see how effective such a technique can be. Beyond Usbek's fuzzy description of what actually happened, readers are obliged to visualize and to create for themselves this sensual encounter of an eager, amorous husband and his timid yet exciting bride:

Do you remember that day? . . . You took a dagger and threatened to immolate a husband who loved you if he continued to demand of you what you loved more than your husband himself. Two months were spent in this struggle between Love and Virtue. You took your chaste scruples too far; you did not give up even after being conquered; right to the very end you defended your dying virginity; you considered me an enemy who had committed an outrage and not a husband who had loved you; you went through a period of three months when you didn't dare look at me without blushing: your obvious confusion seemed to reproach me for having taken advantage of you. Even then I did not experience tranquil possession: you hid from me all you could of your charms and graces and I was drunk with the most liberal favors without having obtained even the smallest ones. (*PL*, 26)

While we might find this passage too long on words and too short on action, Montesquieu's contemporaries brought to such a passage an ability to visualize what is shadowy and an awareness of the implications of the vocabulary. To "surrender" and be "conquered" denoted specific and precise sexual activities. To defend one's virginity evokes an entire combat, during which the military sense of "dying" is enhanced by its sexual meaning of achieving orgasm, at whose climax comes "possession," denoting both the besieging army entering a captured city and a man entering a woman. "Favors" and "graces" were standard clichés for a woman's body, naked and subject to appraisal by an interested male eye. The attraction of scandal and the appeal to prurient interests that this novel held for its first readers should not therefore be overlooked or minimized.

    The epistolary format.   One other element strikes the modern reader as unusual. This novel is written in epistolary format, that is to say, it is composed entirely of letters written by the fictional characters within the novel. No point of view is expressed beyond those presented through the characters who write the letters. Therefore, no one can say with absolute confidence that "Montesquieu is speaking here" or "This represents what Montesquieu thinks." Everything is mediated through the distorting lens of fiction. Before considering *The Persian Letters* as a novel and a work of fiction, I want to examine the very particular conventions of the epistolary genre and see what the implications are for that choice of format.

Letter novels were very popular in the eighteenth century. Indeed, they accounted for a good percentage of all novels published through the first three-quarters of the century. Letters were, we should remember, a most pervasive form of communication and social intercourse. Before telephones, letters were the principal means of communication among people who were not in the same room. To be educated was synonymous with knowing how to read and write letters; private letters were frequently read in public since they contained not only private news intended for the recipient alone but also public news that could be shared with a much wider circle of friends and even mere acquaintances. A hostess could greatly impress her guests by reading them a letter she had just received from some famous correspondent or, indeed, from anyone with something interesting or unusual to report. Such sharing of letters in public continued for almost two centuries in France. Its high watermark stretched at least from Mme de Rambouillet reading the letters of Guez de Balzac in her "Blue Room" to Mme du Deffand reading in her salon those of Voltaire. Letters were like a diary containing raw experiences as they happened and before they could be arranged in some neater (falser and more fictional) fashion. Letters provide immediate, present-tense writing. They do not afford the author the luxury of looking back over his experience and of reshaping it into a more effective story.

In Montesquieu's time letters seemed to be more real and authentic than the kind of third-person omniscient narratives that are considered realistic and objective today. Eighteenth-century readers liked the touch of reality they felt in letters where people spoke of themselves in the first person and of what they themselves had seen, heard, and done. Letters bore witness to real-life experiences in a way that seemed to guarantee truth and veracity. How could you doubt someone who had actually been there? The authenticity of the eyewitness, inherent in the epistolary format, is crucial to the total impact of *The Persian Letters*. The novel's ability to question the status quo, to criticize, and to poke fun at what was happening in France depended on this ability to seem "real." Real foreigners would have a legitimate right to see France differently. Real letters would be a perfectly normal way for these foreigners to communicate their reactions among themselves. Thus Montesquieu chose the perfect vehicle both to bring his ideas before the public and at the same time to disguise their fictional nature. Just as it was natural and commonplace to write letters, it was also eminently possible for such letters to find their way into print in the manner that the anonymous editor in his fictional preface claims:

> I have set these first letters apart to try the public's taste; I have a large number of others in my possession which I could bring forth subsequently. . . . The Persians who are writing here lived with me; we spent our life together. As they regarded me as a man from another world, they hid nothing from me. . . . They gave me most of their letters; I copied them. . . . Therefore I only perform the function of a translator: all my effort has been to adapt this work to our customs. I have spared the reader as much of the Asian language as I could and I have rescued him from an infinite number of hyperboles that would have driven him to the limit. (*PL,* Préface)

This is Montesquieu speaking with tongue firmly in cheek. Nonetheless, deception is part of the whole novel's design. The fact that it was published without the author's name sustains the illusion that these letters were (might have been?) written by foreigners and that they really do represent an outsider's view of French society.

Thus, the epistolary format gave readers a certain assurance of reading real and true letters. Montesquieu reinforces this impression by creating a number of writers and a variety of exchanges. Usbek, of course, dominates the whole; Rica is next in importance, but he is clearly a secondary figure. Many others exist partially, fractionally, in the margins, as it were, of these letters. By refusing to make all the correspondents equal and by not trying to evoke them all in detail, Montesquieu gives an illusion of depth and real-life complexity to his narrative. It is like a painting in which not everyone is seen full-face. Paintings of groups in which everyone stares directly out of the canvas invariably look contrived just as photographs do when their subjects are too consciously posed. In contrast, paintings or photos that show people in action oblivious to the recording artist produce a greater impression of veracity. The irregularity and the very incompleteness of the portrayals argue for their authenticity. Thus, Usbek's wives write to him only a few times. He corresponds with several eunuchs who report to him on the state of the harem. He writes to and receives letters from Ibben, a friend in Smyrna. These extra characters bring some variety to the work and allow Usbek and Rica to focus on different interests when they write back to them. But they are not really individualized. Half-lit and standing in the background, these correspondents nonetheless add a convincing depth to the tableau that keeps Usbek and Rica continually in the foreground.

Since it consists of 161 discrete letters, Montesquieu's novel cannot be a long, continuous narrative.[3] With the notable exception of Letter 141, each letter is short. Only a few run more than two pages in length. Even when several letters are grouped around a single topic, like those on the Troglodytes or population, each letter remains self-contained. Since reading can be done in short bursts with numerous and convenient stopping places, the entire work moves at a rapid and lively pace. The reader never fears fatigue or risks getting lost in a long-winded discussion. This brisk rhythm is accentuated by the constant alternations between the serious and the droll. Montesquieu jumps from topic to topic, from the grave Usbek to the more frivolous Rica, from philosophical discussions about politics and religion to amusing accounts of traffic jams, from analyses of French current events to what was happening in oriental seraglios. We should not underestimate the importance of this bantering tone and this ease of reading when we try to understand the success of the book, which in today's vocabulary could be described as a "crossover hit." *The Persian Letters* captured not only the intellectual market, those readers who were ready to look seriously at the causes and the nature of cultural differences, but also the flighty public that only wanted to be amused and entertained without having to strain its attention span. Montesquieu aimed his book at both these targets.

The Philosophical Issues

This section presents a traditional analysis of the philosophical content of *The Persian Letters*. The subsequent section considers the fictional side of the work. Since this novel is one of the key "philosophical" texts of the eighteenth century, I will use that term in the special sense of relating to the *philosophes* who were the liberal thinkers and writers who brought France's *ancien régime* to the brink of revolution.

Usbek is the character who most frequently addresses the major issues head-on. Early in the novel (*PL,* 11–14) he recounts the story of the Troglodytes and how they struggled to form a viable society. In the beginning, "they were so evil and so ferocious that there was among them no principle of fairness or of justice" (*PL,* 11). Living in continual conflict, they overthrew a king who had conquered them and then the magistrates they themselves had elected. Unable to accept any form of authority, they lived in a state of total but chaotic independence: "all the individuals agreed that they would no longer obey anyone; and that each would look to his own interest without worrying about anyone else's" (*PL*, 11). The Troglodytes achieved absolute liberty but at the price of anarchy. Usbek lists a number of examples of individual selfishness, each of which, although immediately profitable, eventually turned against the originator.

Letter 12 describes two families who escaped from this lawless state where only might made right. Inspired by ideas of humanity, justice, and *virtue* (a term that Montesquieu uses frequently and which must be understood as a civil as well as a moral concept), the two men started a new society: "They worked with shared concern for the common interest." They prospered because they put into practice a civic ideal of good citizenship. They taught their children "that self-interest is always synonymous with the general interest; that the wish to separate oneself from that general interest is to lose oneself; that [civic] virtue is not something that should cost us; that we should not regard it as painful; and that justice for others is charity for ourselves" (*PL*, 12). These Troglodytes were rivals only in doing good deeds. Soon their prosperity provoked the envy of outsiders and they were threatened with invasion. First, they tried to negotiate and maintain peace. When this proved impossible, they defended themselves vigorously. They completely defeated their enemy because they fought not for themselves, selfishly, but generously, for their families and their neighbors. Such an utopia cannot last, however.

The Troglodytes eventually decide to choose a king to rule over them. The most venerable and most just man is selected, but he is disconsolate. He laments that rather than continue to shoulder their individual responsibility to maintain their high level of civic-mindedness and generous cooperation, the Troglodytes now want someone else to tell them what they should do: "In your current situation, having no ruler, you must be virtuous despite yourselves: anything less and you would not be able to survive and you would fall into the misfortunes of your first fathers. But this obligation seems too difficult for you; you prefer to submit to a prince and to obey his laws which would be less demanding than your own customs" (*PL*, 14). At this point the episode abruptly ends. We do not know how the Troglodytes react to the old man's impassioned speech. More important for the moral of the story, we are left in the dark as to the exact consequences of this change of governance although we surmise they will be negative.

This parable contains ideas that will remain basic to all of Montesquieu's subsequent thinking. Laws imposed from the outside cannot create a viable political entity. Only when laws are internalized do they acquire their full effectiveness. The term Montesquieu uses for this inner obligation is *virtue*. Without virtuous citizens, no state can prosper; furthermore, this virtue is a product not of rules and regulations, which again come from the outside, but of personal habits, customs, and a way of living. These mores (*moeurs* in French) create the mind-set that leads to a law-abiding society. Unfortunately, the parable of the Troglodytes does not tell how one can acquire these desirable mores. The founders of the Troglodyte prosperity did teach their children their hard-won and dearly cherished values. Despite that effort, these mores were lost. Along with them disappeared the virtuous republic of self-governing men.

Coming early in the novel and forming the first coherent sequence of letters on a topic of philosophical interest, the Troglodyte episode provides a paradigm of the ideal political state. Around this focal point I would gather, simply for ease of discussion, other remarks scattered throughout the novel on the nature of government and how it functions. Right in the middle, Usbek tries to define the "most reasonable government." According to him, "the most perfect [government] is the one that seeks its end with the least expense; so that the one that leads men in the manner best adapted to their bent and to their inclination is the most perfect" (*PL,* 80). Usbek recognizes that it is most difficult to govern men from the outside. Effective rule plays upon the citizens' own needs and habits. There is no mention of virtue here; indeed, Usbek's stark statement could almost sound totalitarian. The point, however, is that effective government does not run counter to the long-standing customs of its people.

Rica finds that, in matters of fashion, the French despise anything foreign: "whatever is foreign always seems ridiculous to them." But *only* in matters of fashion, for in more important instances, like law, the French import all their thinking: "They have abandoned their ancient laws, made by their first kings in the general assemblies of the nation. . . . they have adopted all the legalities of the popes [canon law] and have made them a new part of their law. . . . These foreign laws have introduced procedures whose excesses are a disgrace to human reason" (*PL,* 100). Because the French forget their own national spirit, their natural and native "inclination," and willingly embrace foreign traditions in jurisprudence, they risk political instability. Here it is difficult not to hear the voice of Montesquieu himself, a provincial lawyer in the Bordeaux Parlement who will become the theoretician of hereditary rights and privileges, harkening back to the oldest native traditions and consistently opposing the innovations of a more powerful centralized administration.

In Letter 129 Usbek explains the limits of legislative effectiveness. Usually legislators are ignorant and follow not reason but their own prejudices and foolish notions. They have confused the power of laws with that of customs. The latter, along with the "national spirit," precede laws and prepare citizens to obey them. To reverse the sequence and to give priority to laws is to misunderstand the real reason why people are law-abiding. Usbek echoes Rica's criticism about France's weakness for importing foreign legislation. The most intelligent legislators, in contrast, are those who have given more authority to families and fathers. By respecting long-standing customs passed down through generations, they allow a natural, internal process of socialization and legalization to take place rather than trying to legislate into action behavior that has not been inculcated into the people as they grow up. Usbek sums up this doctrine in half a phrase: "customs and mores always produce better citizens than laws do" (*PL,* 129). Paternal authority is "the most sacred of all legal powers; it is the only one that does not depend on conventions and that has even preceded them." Fathers are "the very image of the Creator of the Universe."

Liberal thought today would probably disagree with Usbek and prefer a more formalized code over this unrestricted confidence in paternal authority. The comparison itself is no longer in favor: "paternalistic" is usually considered negative when applied to "authority." Basically, however, Usbek's point is that courts cannot enforce laws unless citizens have been educated right from the beginning to accept authority and unless they have a life-style that promotes respect for those laws.

Religion is another topic of major philosophic interest. French *philosophes* almost always opposed official religion—Catholicism in France—because they regarded it as antirational and a source of superstition that exploited human credulity. Montesquieu's presentation of religion is more subtle, avoiding complete condemnation. Whenever he makes a pointed attack against a specific abuse, however, it is all the more effective.

Observing the religious disputes in France, Usbek remarks how little these opponents behave like true Christians and even like good citizens. What he values most in religion is how it helps people to live in society, "for, no matter what religion one practices, respect for laws, love for one's fellow man, devotion to one's parents are always the first acts of religion" (*PL*, 46). Particular dogmas and liturgical practices take a back seat to a civic "golden rule" that preaches respect and harmony. This is a deistic viewpoint, that is to say, a belief that recognizes a personal God but that dictates no specific dogmas or liturgy. Deism turns away from heaven to focus more on earth and on the human interactions necessary for living happily in society. Deism was a radical religious position in the eighteenth century, one that was condemned by the dominant religions. Deism influenced most of our Founding Fathers who, while observing a particular religion as individuals, nonetheless argued for the separation of church and state and refused to establish a state religion. Deism offered tolerance for different beliefs at a time when most religions continued to persecute their rivals as heretical. Usbek closes his letter with the prayer of a religious man who wants to worship God but who refuses to get involved in petty quarrels about specific dogmas: "I cannot so much as move my head without being told that I am offending you; however, I wish to please you and use to that end the life which I hold from you. I do not know if I am mistaken; but I think that the best way to succeed is to live as a good citizen of the society where you have caused me to be born and as a good father of the family that you have given to me" (*PL*, 46). The modest tone should not hide the real strength of this prayer and its determination to live a practical life that holds to the highest ethical and moral standards. Notice how well this type of religion supports the political state. Virtue, as I have already pointed out, is both a moral and a political notion for Montesquieu. In this same spirit of moderation, Usbek recounts a conversation with a priest who echoes the deist's prayer for tolerance and mutual respect: "Zeal itself . . . is often dangerous and it can never be accompanied by too much prudence" (*PL*, 61).

Letter 69 contains a metaphysical discussion of God's attributes and of how they sometimes contradict each other. This passage pinpoints the kind of issues that constitute the petty theological disputes the deist wants to avoid. Similarly, Usbek ends on a note of awe and tolerance that transcends any points of contention: "My dear Rhédi, why so much philosophy? God is so far above us that we cannot even see his clouds. We do not know him at all except in his precepts. He is immense, spiritual, infinite. May his greatness bring us back to our weakness. To show humility always is to adore always" (*PL*, 69).

One of the most quoted letters in the novel is number 97, Usbek's hymn to science and to the achievements of human reason. I will look more closely at it later when I discuss science. Here, however, I have one essential point to make. Although much impressed by science and reason, Usbek does not therefore have to renounce religion. He does not see them as incompatible, or even as necessarily in conflict. In Montesquieu's day, as increasingly in our own, when religion often did oppose scientific progress, this attempt to defuse the quarrel between faith and reason was most important. Usbek separates them because they belong to different spheres and refuses to oppose one with the other: "You will perhaps say that I am speaking too freely about what is most holy among us; you think that this is the fruit of the liberty in which we live in this country [France]. No, thank Heaven, my mind has not corrupted my heart, and as long as I live, Hali will be my prophet" (*PL,* 97). The last line strikes a very personal note. As long as he lived and as much as he found to criticize in the history of the church, Montesquieu remained true to the faith in which he had been born.

Usbek's apparently unobjectionable and innocent religious beliefs hide a sharp two-way sword. By focusing on Islam, Montesquieu can indirectly criticize Christianity. The dangers and shortcomings of religion are not limited to any single sect: criticism of one is often equally valid for the others. While Montesquieu is apparently aiming at the Persian religion, he is able to hit more than one target with the same shot. Usbek writes to Gemchid, his cousin and a cleric, and pities the Europeans who, not being Moslems, cannot attain paradise: "I know that Christians will not go to the home of the Prophets and that the great Hali did not come for them. But, because they have not been lucky enough to have mosques in their countries, do you think that they are condemned to everlasting damnation and that God will punish them for not having practiced a religion which he did not reveal to them?" (*PL,* 35). The belief was widespread among eighteenth-century French Catholics that anyone not belonging to their religion could not be saved. The same belief presented by Usbek seems much less acceptable and even ridiculous. For all its indirectness, Montesquieu's ironic critique is powerful.

Criticism can go beyond these mild bounds. Even before he reaches Europe, Usbek in Letter 18 questions Islam's dietary laws that forbid the eating of pork and other "impure" meats. The answer he receives from his theologian correspondent is so insufficient an answer that it undermines its own viewpoint: it simply self-destructs. The point in dispute, why pork is proscribed, only serves to highlight the arbitrary nature of certain religious beliefs.

Under the cover of his Persian personas, Montesquieu dares to call the pope a "magician" because "sometimes he [the pope] makes the public believe that three is really one, that the bread they eat is not bread, and the wine they drink is not wine, and a thousand other similar things" (*PL,* 24). Usbek is referring, of course, to the mystery of the Trinity, three Persons in one God, and the doctrine of transubstantiation by which bread and wine are changed into Christ's Body and Blood during the mass. These are central doctrines of the Catholic church and Montesquieu is very audacious in signaling them out for ridicule. Rica continues in this same bantering vein with his comments on the fanaticism of the Spanish Inquisition: "for I have heard tell that in Spain and in Portugal there are certain dervishes who can't take a joke and who burn a man as easily as they do straw. . . . Other judges presume that the accused is innocent; these judges always presume he is guilty" (*PL,* 29). Casuistry, or the art of deciding if an action is sinful or not, is ridiculed (*PL,* 57) because some French priests strived for popularity by telling their penitents that nothing they did was wrong. Monasteries and convents are criticized because their members are celibate: Catholic priests, nuns, and monks were not permitted to marry while Protestant clergymen were. In Montesquieu's view, "celibate" meant unproductive. Sterile institutions like the priesthood and various religious orders drained precious resources away from the active and fruitful segments of society: "One finds in every religious house an eternal family where no one is ever born and that keeps going at the expense of every other family. These houses are always open like abysses in which future races are buried" (*PL,* 117). Clearly, this is not exclusively a critique of religion: economic considerations play their part. But this kind of criticism demonstrates that Montesquieu refuses to see any phenomenon in isolation. Religion belongs to a larger context and should be judged for its total impact. In the same letter Usbek condemns the accumulation of wealth by the church: "the dervishes have in their hands almost all the wealth of the nation; they comprise a society of misers who always take and who never give; they amass incessantly income-producing lands so as to acquire more capital. All this wealth becomes, so to speak, paralyzed: no more cash flow, no more commerce, no more arts, no more manufacturing" (*PL,* 117).

The wealth of the church was in fact usually in lands and buildings. Little went into trade or manufacturing, two activities Montesquieu considered essential in a well-balanced state. By removing money from productive uses, the church exercised a deleterious effect on the French economy. Usbek offers in Letter 106 an economic theory based on what might be called gracious living. He refutes the idea that the arts and industry weaken a nation. On the contrary, he indicates, they act as a stimulus running through all social levels, creating needs and increasing production: "Paris is perhaps the most sensual city in the world and the one where pleasure is the most refined; but it is perhaps the one where life is the hardest. So that one man can live luxuriously, one hundred others have to work ceaselessly" (*PL,* 106). This is a percolator metaphor for economic distribution. Wealth is amassed by the rich at the top and trickles down to the working masses at the bottom. The theory is more compatible with eighteenth-century aristocracies than with today's egalitarian democracies. Still, Montesquieu astutely focuses on the need for stimulation to prevent a stagnant economy and on the aggressive competition that keeps a society wealthy: "This desire to work, this drive to get rich, flows from social class to social class, from the skilled workers up to the nobility" (*PL,* 106). He also sees that the flow of money, the exchange of services and products, provides a more important measure of wealth than investments that do not grow and sustain the cycle: "An investment in land only produces for its owner a five percent return; whereas, with one *pistole*'s worth of painting supplies, an artist will produce a canvas that will be worth fifty times its original value" (*PL,* 106). In Montesquieu's economics a powerful and prosperous state will produce luxuries as well as necessities. While Usbek's position is only briefly stated here, he has nonetheless articulated the main lines of an issue that will divide the century. Jean-Jacques Rousseau will argue against luxury in his *Discourses,* claiming that the arts and sciences have spoiled society, while Voltaire will defend it in poems like "Le Mondain" (The worldly sophisticate) where the superfluous becomes a necessity.[4]

The connections among religion, politics, and economics can be seen even more clearly in the letter on the Revocation of the Edict of Nantes. The edict, promulgated by Henri IV in 1598, granted religious freedom to the Protestant minority in France. Believing that a single religion was essential to his government, Louis XIV revoked the edict in 1685. Large numbers of French Protestants, known as Huguenots, fled the country for Switzerland, Holland, and England, weakening France and strengthening the countries that welcomed them. Montesquieu's criticism is indirect since he transposes the situation to Persia and gives it the status of might-have-been. The Persians were lucky enough not to have followed the "blind devotion" that would have eliminated their "most industrious subjects." Usbek draws several conclusions. First, that a strong state should have several religions since "those who practice the tolerated religion are usually more useful to the state than those in the majority religion." Second, that war and conflict come not from the coexistence of several religions but rather from the intolerance generated by a single religion without any alternative: "it is not the multiplicity of religions which caused these wars, it is that spirit of intolerance which inspired the dominant religion; it is that spirit of proselytizing . . . ; it is finally that dizzying spirit whose progress can only be regarded as the entire eclipse of human reason" (*PL,* 85). Montesquieu's anaylsis of the revocation's deleterious economic consequences coincides with that of modern historians.

Since the list of philosophic topics that deserve comment is almost as long as the book itself, it is impossible to do all of them justice here. Suicide provoked controversy throughout the century, with many authors raising philosophical and religious arguments for and against it. Usbek defends the right to commit suicide, arguing that man is but one form of matter in nature and that the whole human race is insignificant and barely worth God's notice: "Do you believe that my body, transformed into a husk of wheat, a worm, or a lawn is changed into a less worthy work of Nature? and that my soul, disengaged from everything terrestrial, has become less sublime?" (*PL,* 76). Usbek hints at a philosophical materialism that will be advanced by others like Diderot and La Mettrie later in the century. By emphasizing that physically man was just another part of nature, materialism challenged the central religious belief that man had a divine soul that elevated him above everything else in nature. Ibben's conventional reply, defending the traditional religious position, offers only a weak rebuttal to Usbek's strong attack. A reader today might even note that Usbek adumbrates modern ecological notions that find value in every niche in the biosphere and that see man as part of the entire life cycle and not as something outside and superior to it.

In the longest sequence of letters on a single topic (112–22) and counterbalancing the Troglodyte episode at the beginning of the novel stand Usbek's thoughts on population, or rather on depopulation. Infant mortality was very high throughout the eighteenth century. Inaccurate censuses left everyone in the dark about the actual population and its real rate of change. For Montesquieu, population was not just a topic of current interest but also a philosophical issue that touched on many other matters. Demographics and religion: the prohibition of divorce and the sterility of monasteries due to clerical celibacy affected birthrates negatively. Demographics and economics: eighteenth-century theories of wealth were closely tied to the size of the population since productivity was a direct function of manpower in an age before the advent of industrialization and the widespread use of machines. Colonies weakened the mother country by enticing away its population and diluting its wealth. Demographics and politics: slaves and their productivity strengthened ancient Rome. In terms of philosophic content, then, population provides the denouement just as the Troglodytes furnished the overture for *The Persian Letters.*

The eighteenth century marked the beginnings of modern science. Usbek writes home to a cleric (the opposition of science and religion is a constant in the book) about those scientists who renounce the poetry of religion for the different, but equally impressive, poetry of science and mathematics: "they have neither heard the ineffable words sounded in the concerts of angels nor felt the formidable grip of divine inspiration; but, left to themselves, deprived of holy marvels, they follow silently along the path of human reason" (*PL,* 97). Without mentioning Newton by name, Usbek pays homage to his discovery of gravity: "They have figured out Chaos and explained, with one simple mechanical principle, the order of the divine architecture." Science speaks to the politician in Usbek since he calls "legislators" those scientists who propose real laws that brook no disobedience and who "only speak to us of general laws, unchanging and eternal, which are observed without exception and with an order, regularity, and infinite rapidity in the immensity of space" (*PL,* 97). Through Usbek we hear Montesquieu's own fascination with universal laws that he sought, not only in science, but also in history and in the conduct of nations. This letter ends with Usbek's pious declaration that the marvels of science have not destroyed his appreciation of religion.

Despite such glowing praise, science is not all good. Misused, it can wreak havoc. Science, after all, did produce the technical advances that made war so devastating. Rhédi reports that "the single invention of bombs had deprived all the peoples of Europe of their liberty" (*PL,* 105). Because of artillery "there is no longer any refuge on earth against injustice and violence." In a sentence that should be taken to heart in an age of mutually assured nuclear destruction, Rhédi says, "I tremble constantly that science might finally succeed in discovering some secret that will provide a quicker way to kill men and to destroy peoples and entire nations" (*PL,* 105). In direct contrast to Usbek's enthusiasm for European science, Rhédi vaunts its opposite: "Happy the ignorance of Mohammed's children!"

Philosophy and science, economics and religion, politics both practical and theoretical are weighty topics indeed. Despite the quick pace and the brevity of these discussions, Montesquieu would probably not have had such a successful novel if those were the only matters he discussed. To balance such serious material he also included light and amusing letters that evoke the daily life of early eighteenth-century France. These deal with the Parisian social whirl and touch on culture (with a small *c*) or on what we might call "life-style."

Rica's first letter gives us a famous picture of traffic jams, high-rise buildings, and the accelerated pace of urban living—all scaled down to eighteenth-century proportions, of course!

Paris is as large as Ispahan. The houses are so high that you would think they are inhabited only by astrologers. You can guess that a city built up in the air, which has six or seven houses each on top of the other, is extremely populous and when everyone goes down into the street, there are some pretty big tie-ups.

You will not believe me perhaps. In the month that I have been here I have not seen a single person walk. . . . they run, they fly. . . . A man who is coming along behind me and passes me, spins me around, and another man, coming from the opposite direction, puts me back in the same place where the first one took me; and I have not traveled one hundred feet but I am more exhausted than if I had traveled ten miles. (*PL*, 24)

Rica also visits a theater and finds that the spectacle takes place in the boxes as well as on stage: the audience is as much on show as the actors are. In a sequence of five letters he visits the library of Saint Geneviève. A monk-librarian gives the guided tour that, while brief, does contain a few noteworthy insights that Montesquieu will develop in subsequent works: "Here are the historians of England, where we see liberty rising ceaselessly out of the flames of discord and sedition; a prince always shaky upon an unshakable throne; an impatient nation, wise even in its fury and who, mistress of the seas (something unheard of until then), mixes business with empire" (*PL*, 134).

Coffee was first introduced into Europe in the late seventeenth century. It became so popular that *cafés*, the French term for coffee, sprang up to serve the drink to an ever-thirsty public. Usbek visits one and experiences its animation: "There is one [café] where they prepare coffee in such a way that it gives wit to those who drink it: at least, among those who are leaving, there is no one who does not think he has four times as much as when he entered" (*PL*, 36). Coffeehouses were noted both for the bizarre individuals one found there (*PL,* 132) and for their brilliant, witty conversation. Usbek overhears part of a literary dispute about Homer and the new translation just published by Mme Dacier, an echo of the long-drawn-out, international controversy known as the quarrel of the Ancients and the Moderns.

Rica meets an alchemist (*PL,* 45) who promises to show him immense riches. He also receives letters from *nouvellistes* (Grub-Street hacks) who "lack only good sense" and whose conversation is based on "a frivolous and ridiculous curiosity" (*PL,* 130). He observes a number of unusual but fascinating phenomena: the mania for gambling among women (*PL,* 56); the laziness and ignorance of judges (*PL,* 68); the distressing cases that come before the law courts (*PL,* 86). Then there are the colorful eccentrics he meets in society: the know-it-alls (*PL,* 72), those who talk constantly (*PL,* 82), the social butterflies who appear all over town (*PL,* 87), and two wits who prepare in advance how to show off their spontaneity (*PL,* 54). What is most impressive in this rapid kaleidoscope of Parisian society is that Montesquieu covers so many different experiences and combines these discrete impressions in a way that produces a total picture of astonishing vividness and completeness.

In a similar vein, current political events leave their traces in these pages. Taking advantage of the regent's liberal regime, Montesquieu pokes fun at the Sun King. "The King of France is old," Letter 37 begins, and he is full of contradictions: "he has a minister who is only eighteen years old and a mistress who is eighty; he loves his religion but cannot abide those who say you must observe it scrupulously; although he flees the bustle of town and does not speak up much, he is busy from morning to night getting people to speak about him; he loves trophies and victories but he fears a good general at the head of his own troops as much as he fears one at the head of an enemy army" (*PL,* 37). While the criticism is not deep, the sardonic tone indicates how quickly the Sun King's glory had tarnished in the six years since his death in 1715. Other political happenings include the exile of the Paris Parlement to Pontoise (*PL,* 140), the news of the death of Louis XIV (*PL,* 92 and 111), public concern about the poor health of the future Louis XV (*PL,* 107), and the continuing quarrel between Jansenists and Jesuits over the papal bull *Unigenitus,* also known as the Constitution (*PL,* 101). As finance minister in 1719, John Law had imagined a scheme to create a national bank and to issue paper money. Both projects were far ahead of their time. After brilliant initial successes, they were swallowed up in the crash that followed frenetic speculation on the stock of Law's India Company. The fortunes won and lost in that debacle shocked the normally stable social and financial hierarchies: "This foreigner has turned the state inside out the way a tailor reverses a garment: he puts on top what was on the bottom, and what was on right he puts on backwards. . . . How many valets are now waited on by their comrades and perhaps tomorrow by their former masters!" (*PL,* 138).

One last subject deserves mention and will serve as a transition to the next section. Western women quite naturally capture the attention of our Persians. Moscow women, it is reported, love to be beaten by their husbands (*PL,* 51), while Parisian women lie about their age (*PL,* 52). Ladies' fashions change rapidly (*PL,* 99), and the intelligence women use for their toilette and their flirtations equals that of a general maneuvering his army (*PL,* 110). French women are unfaithful to their husbands who do not seem overly concerned however (*PL,* 55). In the Persian harem, many women have one lover, while in Paris one woman may have many lovers.

Of course, at the heart of this subject is the juxtaposition, more often implied than stated, of Western and Eastern women. Letter 34 offers an explicit but superficial comparison: Persian women are "more beautiful" while Frenchwomen are "prettier." It continues with a Frenchman's strong condemnation of the harem system, comments that Usbek repeats but does not refute. An equally provocative statement is found earlier (*PL,* 23), when Usbek remarks that, in the West, "women enjoy great freedom." In addition to its social and political perspectives, this novel also contains an important feminine and even feminist element. It belongs within the context of the harem and that erotic, sexual intrigue that opens and closes the narrative. Obviously, the harem is a society that is defined by the way it treats women. Women are not just another source of frivolous anecdotes. How they are treated is a topic of the highest philosophic importance. The tension between the freedom of Frenchwomen and the position of Persian women confined to their harem is one of the elements best depicted by the fictional portion of *The Persian Letters.*

The Novel

Years after the remarkable success of *The Persian Letters,* Montesquieu wrote in the preface to the new edition of 1754 that the book was "une espèce de roman," "a kind of novel." But the phrase is provocative and ambiguous. It can additionally signify a novel of an uncertain nature, or even an incomplete or misformed novel. Only in the past 20 years have critics begun to consider *The Persian Letters* as a legitimate novel. Their discussions have centered around two phrases that were never taken seriously for over two centuries, the "espèce de roman" just quoted and the following sentence: "the author seized the advantage of being able to mix philosophy, politics, and morality together with a novel, and to unify the whole with a secret, and in a certain sense, unnoticed chain" ("Quelques Réflexions"). Critics who have sought this "secret chain" often claim to find it in the harem intrigue.[5] Here I will offer a reading of *The Persian Letters* that takes its novelistic elements seriously, especially the depiction of the oriental seraglio and what happens behind its closed doors.

To see Montesquieu's book principally as a novel requires a new attitude toward the text itself. The traditional attitude is that the book contains information of a philosophical, political, or social nature and that this material can be excerpted from the whole. Numerous anthologies and editions treat the text in precisely this fashion. Usbek's account of the Troglodytes is one major example. It is frequently quoted and then connected to Montesquieu's thought about political responsibility as seen in *The Spirit of the Laws*. Such selective reading is very tempting; indeed, it is the kind of analysis I offered in the last section.

If, however, the book is to be read as a novel, then it must be read as a whole with all its parts examined for their contribution to the overall effect. This would argue against taking incidents out of context since that context determines how readers should understand each particular incident. Earlier I said that the epistolary format obliged Montesquieu to speak not in his own voice, as he would do later in the *Laws,* but rather in the voices of the fictional characters he creates. True, Usbek does resemble Montesquieu. They are both interested in the same topics, and both attempt to understand the deeper causes of the phenomena they observe. Usbek is criticized by his friend Rustan in terms that Montesquieu must have heard applied to himself later in life as he drifted from his office in the Bordeaux Parlement toward his other interests: "No one understands how you can leave your wives, your family, your friends, and your country to go into regions unknown to Persians" (*PL,* 5). Yet Montesquieu is more than Usbek, which is perhaps another way of saying that Usbek is less than Montesquieu. To equate them completely with each other diminishes Montesquieu too much. Furthermore, Montesquieu also resembles the flighty Rica who is an obvious foil for the serious Usbek. Both Montesquieu and Rica love to frequent the fashionable drawing rooms and the salons of Regency Paris. Both are keen observers of women and devote a good deal of their time talking to and about them. Montesquieu cannot then be identified exclusively with, and thus limited to, any one of his characters. He remains the author who created them all and who placed them within a complex web of interactions.

My point is that we cannot refer to *The Persian Letters* simply as an early draft of the *Laws*. In the latter work, Montesquieu has invented no fictional vehicle to present his ideas; in the former, he has. Consequently, we must factor this fictional element into our final interpretation. We should not think that whatever Usbek says is exactly what Montesquieu means. Precisely because it is a fiction, an invention, a creation of the author's mind, the novel provides a vast arena for irony. In the multiplicity of the competing voices that advance sometimes contradictory opinions, no one can always and automatically identify Montesquieu's final thought. In short, Usbek is not infallible and readers must be constantly attentive to the possibility that Montesquieu is distancing himself from his hero. The fictional element is not, then, a sugarcoating, a facile trick to dupe the public into swallowing a healthy dose of information they would have spurned under any other form. Rather, the fiction is part and parcel of Montesquieu's investigation. This novel describes a seeking after knowledge, and not the distribution of knowledge already acquired.

This is not to say that novel and philosophy are incompatible. Far from it. What must be done, however, is to read the philosophy in the light of the fiction. The story surrounding the harem, for example, touches upon some of the major issues discussed in the previous section as philosophy: the nature of government, the relationship between subjects and rulers, the struggle between new knowledge and old customs.

The eunuchs in Usbek's seraglio behave like bad legislators. They are tyrants who rule through fear and who treat their subjects like slaves. The irony here is enormous since the eunuchs are themselves slaves while the subjects they abuse so thoroughly are the wives of their absolute ruler! In an early letter, one too often overlooked, the First Eunuch candidly confesses how much he detests the women he rules over and how he derives a sadistic pleasure from the power he wields:

I look on women with indifference and I throw back at them all their scorn and all the torments they have made me suffer. I always remember that I was born to rule over them and it seems that I become a man again whenever I command them. I hate them. . . . the pleasure of being obeyed gives me a secret joy: when I deprive them of everything, it seems that it's for myself and I always derive an indirect satisfaction from it. I find myself in the harem as in a small empire, and my ambition, the only passion I retain, can be somewhat satisfied. (*PL,* 9)

The impotent and sexless male recovers his virility and sense of power only when he is able to oppress another. In Montesquieu's Persia (and in his France, too), even relatively powerless men can exert their authority over women, who were rarely more than second-class citizens. The eunuch's words are disquieting for all the class and sexual hatred they contain as well as for the connections they suggest between sexuality and power, pleasure and pain. In the middle of the novel, Usbek receives a letter from the Head Black Eunuch that warns him of dissensions in the harem. This letter adumbrates the final revolt that will close the novel and call Usbek back home. For the moment, however, it describes only chaos and confusion: "the seraglio is in total disorder and frightful confusion; war reigns among your wives; your eunuchs are divided; one hears only complaints, only murmurings, only reproaches" (*PL,* 64). Anarchy reigns in this society because the ruler has lost touch with the nature of his true authority and because he is too distant from both his ministers and his subjects. Usbek's harem is a society in crisis. The harem world's continuous internecine disputes and the unmitigated opposition of egotistical self-interests are exactly the same characteristics that define the bad Troglodytes and explain why their state failed. The Head Eunuch regrets the old days when society was run along totalitarian lines: "The First Eunuch, the most severe man I have ever seen in my life, governed it with absolute authority. One heard no talk of divisions or of quarrels: a profound silence reigned everywhere. . . . the slightest refusal to obey was punished without mercy" (*PL,* 64). The eunuch government is clearly despotic, allowing no discussion among its subjects, running everything from its own single-minded perspective. The Head Black Eunuch sees Usbek's love and kindness as the cause of disorder. He begs permission to reinstate the iron rule of power and force: "if . . . you allowed me [the option] of punishing; if, instead of letting yourself be moved by their pleas and their tears, you sent them to cry before me, I, who am never moved, I would soon fit them to the yoke they should bear and I would wear down their haughty and independent manner" (*PL*, 64). The Head Black Eunuch sees mercy as poor government. Recognizing no excuses and tolerating no variation from his straight-and-narrow line, this eunuch prefers the quick application of punishments that would impose duty and obedience like a "yoke" that citizens must bear painfully. The choice of metaphor speaks volumes, albeit indirectly, about the eunuch's political conviction that the women in the harem should be treated like beasts and not like fellow human beings.

Thus, examination of various forms of government is not confined to the philosophical reflections of Usbek and Rica. The fictional seraglio also serves to illustrate how governments function. Usbek's harem exhibits the same flaws and characteristics that Montesquieu would later describe as despotic in the *Laws*. This temptation to rule tyrannically, to resort to power rather than to persuasion, to force obedience rather than to elicit cooperation, is too strong to resist. At the end of the novel, when disorder breaks out again, Usbek reverts to brute force rather than to any more intelligent exercise of authority. He writes to his eunuchs: "Receive by this letter unlimited power over all the seraglio: give orders with as much authority as myself. Let fear and terror walk with you" (*PL*, 148). Thus Usbek approves the tyranny advocated by the Head Black Eunuch and proves himself a most unenlightened despot.

Governing his harem is both a personal and a philosophical dilemma for Usbek; it might even be considered a tragedy. In the course of his travels in France he has become an enlightened *philosophe*. He discourses knowingly about the best forms of government. He understands why societies can be corrupted and he explains on a number of occasions how this disintegration comes about. He almost seems to know how to avoid the pitfalls. But all that concerns life in the abstract. In his personal life, he is a dismal failure. Early in the novel Usbek scolds one of his wives, Zachi, because she has broken one of the harem's rules and thus offended his honor. He goes on paradoxically to defend the harem as a liberating place and his own authoritarian behavior as freedom:

What would you then do if you could leave this holy place which is for you a hard prison just as it is for your companions a sweet refuge against the attacks of vice, a holy temple where your sex loses its weakness and becomes invincible despite your natural deficiencies? What would you do if, left to yourself, you had as a defense only your love for me, which is so grievously offended, and your duty, which you have so shamelessly betrayed? Oh how the customs of

the country where you live are holy because they snatch you from the attacks
of the vilest slaves! You should thank me for the restrictions I place upon you
since it is only through them that you deserve to continue living. (*PL, 20*)

Usbek is himself a prisoner of his upbringing and the thinking of his
culture. He finds the injustice of his household to be normal and even
praises these customs. His denigration of women and of their intrinsic
human value is reprehensible. A true despot, he sees himself as the
center of the universe. His wives have value and thus deserve to live
only because of their subservience to him. Such monstrous egotism is
Usbek's other face, that of the petty tyrant who does not hesitate to
declare his absolute and unquestionable authority over the eunuchs who
are the ministers of his policies in terms that he could just as easily have
used to describe his power over Zachi and his other wives: "And who
are you but lowly tools that I can break at a whim; you who exist only
as long as you obey; you who are in this world only to live under my
laws or to die as soon as I command it; you who breathe only as long
as my happiness, my affection, even my jealousy have need of your
lowliness; and finally you who cannot have any lot but submission, any
soul but my desire, any hope but my felicity?" (*PL, 21*). What a
revealing expression of the totalitarian mind-set! What selfish despotism! What blindness to the human worth of others! What an
effective illustration of the axiom that power corrupts the soul! And let
us remember, this comes from the pen of Usbek whom some would
equate with Montesquieu himself.

   As solid as this tyrannical power seems, it is weak and unstable,
corrupted at its base. Although an absolute ruler, Usbek depends on
his eunuchs to carry out his will. While totally subject to their master,
these eunuchs nonetheless have their own agenda for wielding power
and take out their personal and institutional frustrations on those below
them. The women in the harem occupy a position of ostensible privilege
as wives of the ruler and yet they suffer injustice at the hands of their
inferiors, their husband's slaves. They are isolated from any meaningful
activity just as they are separated both by the eunuchs and physical
distance from the man who holds their fate in his hands. His affection
for them has no stable basis and always takes second place to his own
sense of honor and privilege. Montesquieu captures this volatile mixture
of power and weakness, love and hatred, sex and politics in the harem
that he locates on the margins both of his philosophical treatise and his
randy oriental tale.

Looking at *The Persian Letters* as a novel and not just a philosophical or sociological treatise forces us to acknowledge such complexities deep in the fabric of the text. Usbek's authoritarian arrogance provokes the revolt of the slave–wives led by Roxane. Her letter which closes the novel contains a ringing declaration of her independence. She rejects the notion that she exists solely for Usbek's pleasure or that he might control her inner life as he does her external behavior: "How could you have thought me foolish enough to believe that I existed in the world only to adore your whims? . . . No, I might have lived in slavery, but I was always free!" (*PL*, 161). Roxane's revolt has been crushed by the eunuchs, however. To escape from them and from Usbek, she has poisoned herself, an unforeseen application of the right to suicide that Usbek had defended earlier. Her final revelations oblige us to reread one of Usbek's letters and to revise our interpretation of it. Earlier I cited Letter 26 as an illustration of the novel's erotic content: the scene of lovemaking between an ardent husband and his demurring wife. Now we understand the situation differently. Roxane's resistance did not stem from timidity as Usbek erroneously thought. She was betraying her invincible horror at being his slave, his plaything, his object. The shy reserve that so excited Usbek was in fact her stubborn desire to preserve her freedom. Sexual and political power are two sides of the same coin. In this despotic harem, the husband is tyrant, his wife a slave, and love a combat of wills that determines who will dominate whom. Seeing Roxane menacing him with a dagger aroused Usbek sexually. He remained blissfully unaware of the true motive behind her gesture while she resisted his sexual advances because she fully understood their political underpinning. As we read deeper into the text as a novel, we find that Roxane was fighting, and eventually dying, for a freedom that was both sexual and political.

As this example illustrates, fiction by its very nature does not function in the same straightforward way as a philosophical essay. The simple fact that all this novel's action is presented through letters whose writers are subjective and limited in their point of view renders any effort to find a stable or reliable focus problematic. In addition to such ironic undercutting, Montesquieu's epistolary novel also plays with other effects like fragmentation and juxtaposition that are more proper to fiction than the essay.

Short, but rich in specific details, these letters resemble the sound bites so dear to television newscasting. Topics appear and disappear quickly. They strike our imagination and grab our attention only mo-

mentarily because they are never treated in enough depth to constitute
a satisfying whole. As bits and pieces flash rapidly before our eyes,
juggled in no easily apparent order of exposition, these letters re-create
the jumble we experience when we observe events from too close. Montesquieu's intention is precisely to dazzle us with these fragments by
presenting them so rapidly and incompletely. He emphasizes this fragmentation by using jump cuts rather than smooth transitions between
topics. In more traditional terms, parataxis is the principal rhetorical
device: Montesquieu suppresses the connections so that each subject is
highlighted by its isolation. Each letter or each paragraph (the rate of
fragmentation and the tempo increase as more topics are presented
within the same space) introduces a new personage, a different adven-
ture, another encounter. Letters themselves are paratactic. They are
discrete, self-contained units, distinguished by different writers, different recipients, and different subjects except in rare sequences like those
devoted to the Troglodytes or population. Printed and read separately,
they are cut off from each other, fragmented pieces whose connections
and coherence become evident only much later, if ever.

   Although the letters follow no logical sequence in terms of the subjects treated, that does not mean they are ordered randomly or hap-
hazardly. On the contrary, they are often juxtaposed with acute
intelligence, producing glaring contradictions and illogical connections
that demand further analysis. Letter 148, in which Usbek delegates
unlimited power to his eunuchs follows closely his cogent analysis of
ministers (PL, 146) and how they, through their example, can corrupt
an entire nation by their misbehavior and their bad example. Immediately after the sequence on the Troglodytes appears a letter from one
eunuch to another discussing authority: "I thought I saw you undergo
a second birth and quit one servitude where you always had to obey for
another servitude where you had to rule. I took charge of your education" (PL, 15). Letter 14 stopped open-ended with the dilemma of
whether the Troglodytes would choose a ruler or continue to live by the
higher standards of their conscience and customs. Letter 15 follows
with talk of one tyrant grooming another, one despot preparing his suc-
cessor in that most vile political system, the rule of eunuchs over im-
prisoned women. Thus two strategies proper to fiction, fragmentation
and juxtaposition, enrich the text by making it unstable, ambiguous,
and provocative, all at the expense of discursive clarity. Philosophic
points are no longer expressed clearly; they are refracted, rendered more
complex, more disturbing by their fictional presentation.

Again taking advantage of fiction's freedom to be indirect and opaque, Montesquieu favors allusions over direct statements, what is slightly off-center over anything immediately and easily comprehensible. Often a letter begins by addressing one topic and then suddenly switches to another. The real subject of the letter is only indirectly related to that initial jumping-off point. The reader can never be sure what the letter is really about until it is over. This accounts for a good part of the novel's seemingly endless variety. Since the letters are almost always short, they never exhaust their subjects. By leaving issues up in the air, Montesquieu in effect refuses to offer solutions. Straightforward answers are not provided. Controversy is evoked, a position is staked out, but there is no guarantee that any single statement is the correct one. Even the serious Usbek comes close to contradicting himself. His long praise of rational science in Letter 97, for example, ends in a pious reaffirmation of his religious faith. When done in this fashion fiction can both underlie and undermine philosophy.

Reading *The Persian Letters* is not therefore the frivolous recreational reading that we might have suspected from its enormous success, its oriental disguise, and its erotic flavor. Readers are called upon to bring their own intelligence and knowledge of current events to the novel or else the references to the Law debacle, the exile of Parlement, the latest happening at the Académie Française or the Sorbonne will be lost. To appreciate the play of ideas, the reader must actively complete the suggestions offered by the text. Similarly, the allusive presentation of subject matter requires an attentive and alert reader who cooperates with the text. Reading cannot be lackadaisical or passive; on the contrary, it must be active, making connections not readily apparent at first and judging each piece of the puzzle by its relationship to all the others.

Such demands on the reader make for a rich novel but a weak essay or treatise. When reflections are scattered throughout the text with no indication that they should be read together, it is admittedly difficult to recognize relationships, identify the proper contexts, and deduce the correct interpretations. This difficulty is complicated by the comic attitude of some correspondents. Any analysis of Montesquieu's ideas, including my own in the previous section, runs the risk of being faulted for its necessarily heavy-handed treatment of such slippery material. Usbek's Troglodytes are presented with due seriousness, but Rica's Spain is largely a caricature with, nonetheless, a few telling criticisms and incisive remarks. How to weigh such variables? That, too, depends on the readers and the arguments they can find to support their interpretations. In any case, we are warned that we cannot accept this novel at face value. Rather we must understand it as a complex entity turning back on itself, now contradicting, now reinforcing earlier positions. Such complex internal workings characterize not the expository essay, but the work of fiction.

Once we accept *The Persian Letters* as a conscious work of fiction, it follows that the author arranged the letters in an order that he considered most effective. The final letters, for example, which deal with the seraglio's revolt, are all grouped together (*PL,* 147–61) even though this interrupts the chronology the novel has respected up to this point. Letter 146 was written three years later (November 1720) than Letter 147 which is dated September 1717 ("Rhegab" according to Montesquieu's pseudo-calendar). In one sense this failure to respect normal chronology might be construed as an effort toward creating greater realism. Letters are out of strict order because Montesquieu wants to take into account the time lag involved in the long passage of the letters from Persia to Paris. This would be consistent with Montesquieu's efforts to construct a viable Persian calendar for dating the letters.[6]

But there are other, better interpretations for these curious and provocative time distortions.[7] While Usbek writes one of his most despotic letters back to Persia in February (Letter 148, "Let fear and terror walk with you"), he is also capable of producing the very philosophic sequence on European population (*PL,* 113–22) only a few months later, in October and November 1718. The letters written in May 1720 in which Roxane inspires the wives to revolt against the eunuchs and then commits suicide, arrive in late October or November just as Usbek discourses (in Letter 146) about the role of ministers in the state. The juxtaposition by dates of such contradictions is both striking and invisible. Striking because this discrepancy reveals that Usbek has failed miserably to make enlightened wisdom a part of his personal life. Yet invisible because the juxtaposition is not obvious: the reader is left to figure it out alone and to bring together letters separated by the text itself.

The harem revolt as reported in the last 15 letters spans two years. The first indications of the growing sedition were written by the eunuchs in 1718 while Roxane's unanswered final letter is dated May 1720. Grouped together and thus violating the strict chronology that preceded, these final letters stand as a block respecting an impulse more powerful than mere temporal sequence. Printed as a dramatic unit, these letters proclaim the art of fiction at work. They force the reader to experience the precipitation, the chaos, and the shock of those final events. The harem intrigue closes with a rush, telescoping events that cover two long years into a few pages. The effect is striking and it is also supremely literary, the triumph of an emotional impact over a more logical but much weaker ending. The fictional order magnifies the dramatic climax that would have been lost had the letters remained in their real time sequence. Such an obviously arranged disposition, peaking with the high drama, even the tragedy, of Roxane's suicide, argues in favor of a "secret chain" and the artistic arrangement proper to a novel.

My remarks on chronology would not be complete without also mentioning Usbek's silence during the final phase of the novel. Out of the total of 161 letters, Usbek writes 75, or about half. While he produces 67 of the first 124 letters (more than half the total), he authors only 8 of the last 37. Clearly the garrulous Usbek who dominates the novel by the power of his word falls curiously silent in its final quarter.

Usbek the philosopher is literally worlds apart from Usbek the husband and tyrant. The clash between these two aspects of his temperament is underlined by his growing silence. Usbek's mutism, which demonstrates the paradoxical coexistence of the *philosophe* and the despot, does not become evident in real time. On the contrary, only the highly dramatic, forced perspective of the final letters reveals (even more: it creates) this silence. What else is the secret chain but the author's clever arrangement of material so as to produce an effective climax? As Usbek loses his harem, he also loses his power over words and his ability to dominate the novel just as he dominated his wives and his harem. For three-quarters of the novel he has been able to judge, analyze, and understand the complex social phenomena he witnesses. Now his authority evaporates, either as ruler and husband or as cultural critic and observer. Perceptive, perspicacious, and rational in so many areas, Usbek reacts instinctively and not intelligently to the crisis at home. He cannot escape from his upbringing as an Eastern tyrant. He discards the hard-won wisdom of nine years in the West as he reverts to the despotic behavior of his native land. Fittingly, the novel's last word belongs not to Usbek but to Roxane. In defeat she triumphs, just as Usbek, who has been winning all along as the directing intelligence and the vocal focus of the novel, quite clearly loses.

Usbek's presence throughout this epistolary novel has been quite literally verbal. He exists only because he writes: by its very format and logic an epistolary novel creates characters only when they write. Usbek dominates his correspondents and his readers by virtue of his word, his ability to speak and to write. Indeed, it is precisely his eloquence that has led so many to confuse him with Montesquieu. That verbal power slips away from him as the novel ends. Silent and defeated, he returns home, but to a home that no longer exists because he has destroyed it by the word he sent to his eunuchs to punish his wives.

Although Usbek does not believe that love would be more effective than terror in governing, more insightful readers will remember the lesson contained in the Persian story Rica sent him in Letter 141. As the longest single letter in the novel it demands special attention. Its position just before the outbreak of the harem catastrophe marks it as a last-minute warning to Usbek. Unfortunately, Usbek, on the brink of losing his power to speak, also proves incapable of listening. Perhaps he, like so many other readers, does not think that fiction can convey important philosophical truths.

In a seraglio ruled by terror and jealousy, disgruntled women are prepared to die in order to escape. When divine intervention substitutes for the old tyrant Ibrahim a new husband who trusts his wives and believes in their virtue, they give him both their love and their fidelity. When the tyrant returns, he is driven from the harem by his former wives who now enjoy freedom and equality with a new master they voluntarily choose to respect and honor. The political moral seems evident. Both the vocabulary and the ideas recall the situation and thus the lesson of the Troglodytes. This fable of women running and ruling their own lives, a happy harem story, echoes that other utopia, the parable of the Troglodytes ruled by good example and civic virtue. Both episodes stand at the margins, near the beginning and the end of the novel, bracketing the philosophical issues in-between. From their commanding positions they demonstrate how fictions can effectively speak about good government.

Despite the knowledge he has acquired during his long travels, Usbek cannot make a radical break with the culture that fashioned him. Therefore he does not belong outside the discussion that Montesquieu undertakes on questions of politics and mores like a disembodied observer. On the contrary, he is an integral part of that discussion and even its principal example.

The Persian Letters which at times seems so light and frothy contains a dark and serious side. The obstacles that true enlightenment will have to overcome are imposing. If Usbek's case is at all typical, the chances of success are slim indeed. The paradox of man's ability to reason and his inability to act according to that reason, which is so well illustrated by Usbek's penetrating intelligence and his tragic blindness, is still not resolved today. Montesquieu's novel justifies its past success and modern value not just because of its philosophical content but also, and perhaps more importantly, because of its ironic undercutting and constant questioning of those very philosophical ideas.

Chapter Three
Voyages in Europe

On 5 April 1728 Montesquieu left Paris and began a trip through Europe that would last three years. This voyage had a profound effect on Montesquieu's thinking. His personal, first hand contact with Italy left its impression on the *Considerations on the Causes of the Greatness of the Romans and their Decadence* while his experiences in England bore fruit in *The Spirit of the Laws*. In addition to those major publications, his three years of travel filled several volumes of notebooks or travel diaries that he kept to record his impressions.

These travel journals bear several titles corresponding to their subject matter: *Voyage en Autriche* (Trip to Austria), the *Voyage de Gratz à La Haye* (Trip from Gratz to The Hague), which is the most extensive and concerns Italy in particular, and the *Notes sur l'Angleterre* (Notes on England). The *Notes* first found their way into print in 1818, but the other texts were not printed until 1894–96. Editors usually group under the rubric *Voyages* other related writings, for example, a fuller and more complete version of his experiences in Genoa ("Lettre sur Gênes") and Florence ("Florence"). Essays on the interconnection of weather, eating habits, and mores, "Réflexions sur la sobriété des habitants de Rome" (Reflections on the sobriety of the inhabitants of Rome), as well as art and aesthetics, "De la mainère gothique" (On the Gothic style), both derive from these travel notebooks.

Although these journals were not published during Montesquieu's lifetime, he did have them recopied during the years 1749–53. They are not finished in the same sense that his published works are, even though evidence indicates that the texts were reworked after their "on-the-spot" composition. Despite the recopying and the revisions that might have been made at that time, these notebooks are very much the product of a man on the move. They are not, for example, always chronologically correct. On occasion Montesquieu has added subsequent reflections (how much later we do not know: a few days, weeks, years?) to the original account of his daily activities. There are numerous lacunae, like that very active year in England for which all materials except the rather brief *Notes* have been lost.

Despite their incomplete nature, Montesquieu's journals reveal him as a typical eighteenth-century traveler. Unvarnished and natural, he sees the sights during that obligatory piece of old-regime education, the grand tour. He is collecting and storing here the raw data of experience that will become, in other writings and in more polished formats, his considered judgment on issues that interested him.

Itinerary

Montesquieu's itinerary is known in many of its small details,[1] although the departure and initial stages of the trip have left no trace. His account begins in late May 1728 when he reached Vienna, the capital of the Hapsburg empire. He visited the emperor, Charles VI, at his hunting lodge in Laxenburg, and Prince Eugene at the Bellevedere, his chateau and gardens in present-day Vienna. Before setting off for Venice on 12 August, where he would spend a month, he made an excursion into Hungary to visit the mines at Kremnitz, Schmnitz, and Neu-Sohl. This side trip was recorded separately in his "Mémoires sur les mines" (Memoirs on mines), which were written after his return to France and read before the Academy of Bordeaux in 1731. He passed through the Venetian states of Padua and Verona to arrive at Milan on 24 September. From there he visited the area around Lake Como. Having pushed as far west as Turin (23 October), he turned south to Genoa (9 November), Pisa (24 November), and Florence (1 December). He arrived in Rome on 19 January 1729. He took a side trip to Naples from 18 April until 11 May. On 4 July, after a total sojourn of some six months in the Eternal City, he departed northeast toward the Adriatic coast and the city of Loretto. He then moved northward, reaching Bologna (9 July), Modena (17 July), Parma, and Mantua (27 July). After revisiting Verona, he crossed the Alps through the Brenner Pass and entered the Tyrol. On 30 July he arrived in Trent in lower Bavaria. On 3 August (erroneously noted by Montesquieu as 3 July) he arrived in Munich, and on 16 August in Augsburg. From there he traveled to Kannstad near Stuttgart, and then on to Louisburg and Heilbronn.

Traveling through the Rhone valley, Montesquieu reached Heidelberg (25 August), Mannheim (26 August), and Cologne (8 September). On 24 September he arrived in Hanover whose elector had gone to rule over England as George I in 1714. The British crown had passed to the House of Hanover following the death of Queen Anne. The then-reigning English monarchs, George II and Queen Caroline, had ascended the throne in 1727. On 12 October he was in Utrecht and on 15 October

in Amsterdam. In Holland he met Lord Chesterfield, the English ambassador, who accompanied him to England. They left on 31 October
1729 from The Hague in Chesterfield's own yacht.

Montesquieu's account of the English portion of his trip is quite
abbreviated because the pertinent volumes of his travel journals have
been lost. A grandson living in England in the nineteenth century
burned a number of documents and manuscripts dating from this visit.
Thus we have only a few incidents on record, like his attendance at
Parliament in January 1730. Nonetheless, we can be sure Montesquieu
was influenced by what he did and saw in Britain. His mature reflections on the English political system constitute a famous chapter in *The
Spirit of the Laws*. We also know that he was inducted into the Royal
Society in February 1730 and into the Freemasons in May of that same
year. Thanks to friends and his own international reputation, he met
many of the leading statesmen and scholars of the time.

It is not known exactly when Montesquieu left England. Perhaps it
was in December 1730. After a stop in Paris, during which he seems
to have attended a meeting of the Académie Française, he returned to
La Brède in May 1731.

Travel Themes

For the sake of analysis I will break down my examination of the
travel writings into five large categories or themes. This method will
enable me to impose greater coherence on the discussion while also
allowing me to focus on the most significant details of Montesquieu's
trip.

Geography offers the initial category for my analysis. More than
most other eighteenth-century writers, Montesquieu in these pages is
alive to the land he travels through and the people he sees. My simple
enumeration of cities, stopping places, and dates gives some feel for
travel conditions two centuries ago. Other passages bear witness to the
rigors and pace of eighteenth-century transportation: "It's twenty-four
German miles from Vienna to Gratz. At Schottwein you begin to climb
a high mountain called Semmering. Thanks to the work done there and
the winding of the road, you climb it almost imperceptibly. In the past
it required six oxen to each carriage and two hours to get up there; now,
with two horses, you do it in half an hour."[2] Even for a first-class
voyager like the président, travel was an arduous business.

Geography includes questions of terrain. Seeking out vantage points that today would be called aerial views, Montesquieu attempted to get a perspective that Georges Van Den Abbeele has analyzed as a paradigm of his intellectual method:[3] "Whenever I arrive in a city, I always go to the highest steeple or the highest tower in order to see everything as a whole before seeing its parts; and, on leaving, I do the same, to clarify my ideas" (*VE*, 259–60). Always the analytical Cartesian, Montesquieu first tries to grasp the full extent or scope of his subject. Then he divides it into appropriate parts for better investigation and finally attempts to reintegrate those partial bits of knowledge into a comprehensible but now reorganized whole.

Although more classical than romantic in his sensibility, and therefore lacking the romantic feel for nature, Montesquieu is nonetheless very conscious of the topography and the physical nature of the different sites he visits. In his "Lettre sur Gênes" (Letter on Genoa), he describes that port and its coastline in vivid and precise detail. He takes a boat trip on the Bay of Naples and carefully describes what he sees. He draws the floor plan of the castle at Louisburg and a map of Mannheim. He invariably notices the strategic position and fortifications of a city like Brunswick or the commercial value of Savoy's location as a junction and transit point between France and Italy. Reflecting on the Brenner Pass, he says, "The quality of the government and the passage of men and merchandise make it comfortable to live in the Tyrol despite nature. . . . The Tyrol is a natural fortress that cannot be captured. Peasants with rocks would defeat an army" (*VE*, 307c).

Climate is related to geography. Montesquieu is especially curious about the quality of the air and its effect on people wherever he goes. He pondered the complexities of a seasonal atmospheric condition in Rome, called the *intempérie*, which was responsible for serious illness, probably malaria, and various other (albeit less serious) physical reactions.

Second, the baron de la Brède was an educated tourist who was making the grand tour for its cultural value. The tour was an eighteenth-century institution made famous especially by young Englishmen seeing the Continent. It provided the finishing touch to a gentleman's education through firsthand contact with architecture and art, especially the great paintings of the Italian Renaissance. We must remember that there was no way to see, literally, works of art in the eighteenth century unless one visited them personally. No inexpensive reproductions, no postcards, and no slides were on sale at the local bookstore, nor did art books with accurate plates exist then as they do now. The grand tour provided what was often the single opportunity of a lifetime to experience these great paintings.

Huge blocks of Montesquieu's time were dedicated to the patient and thoughtful inspection of the old masters. In a Milan church he was able to see "in the refectory, the famous painting of Leonardo da Vinci, which is a *Last Supper*. . . . You see life, movement, astonishment in the four groups of twelve Apostles; all the passions of fear, sorrow, astonishment, affection, doubt; Judas's surprise is mixed with impudence. . . . in all, it is one of the beautiful paintings of the world" *(VE,* 233c). A few pages later he adds some remarks that he forgot to include before or that perhaps represent new information he has gathered after his initial visit: "The picture of Leonardo da Vinci . . . is painted on the wall, in oil, with, on top, a varnish that no one knows how to reproduce; because of that, no one paints on walls anymore except in fresco" *(VE,* 234c). Such a passage demonstrates the insouciant composition of the notebooks. Montesquieu does not feel compelled to group his comments or to exhaust each subject before continuing. He writes as he travels, in a perpetual present tense of experience. He records what he sees as he sees it, and in so doing captures the spontaneity of his experience.

Of all the painters he saw, the one he incontestably rated the best was Raphael. Whenever he had an opportunity, Montesquieu contemplated Raphael's paintings with unflagging admiration. He devotes several pages to a description and evaluation of the gallery that Raphael painted in the Farnese Palace in Florence. In the Vatican he waxes enthusiastic over another of Raphael's masterpieces: *"Primo,* Raphael's Loggia, what a divine and admirable work! What accurate draftsmanship! What beauty! What naturalness! This is not painting, this is nature itself. . . . Finally, it seems that God uses Raphael's hand to create" *(VE,* 267c). In his discussion of a number of painters and of Raphael especially, Montesquieu reveals an acute artistic judgment and an innate aesthetic sense.[4] The enthusiasm and the excitement he expresses as he contemplates great art speaks eloquently of the value of this trip and of the deep impressions he would bring back to La Brède from Italy.

Another, similar, aspect of the grand tour involved visiting libraries, archives, and other academically oriented institutions that housed collections of various kinds that would interest intellectuals. The latter included *cabinets de curiosités,* private accumulations of rare and unusual artifacts that were the distant ancestors of our museums of natural history. Montesquieu visiting the Ambrosino Library in Milan recalls Rica making a similar visit in *The Persian Letters*. While in Turin, he saw in the archives an ancient Egyptian relic, a stone tablet of Isis; in the cathedral, the Holy Shroud. In Bologna, the Institute is a typically eighteenth-century combination of scientific interests, half museum and half planetarium, containing among other "curiosities" "rare birds from America and elsewhere; rare fish; a pile of bird nests ingeniously built, with their eggs; a heap of marine plants; another one of sea shells; a pile of all sorts of metal ores, tin, copper, gold, silver, lead; a pile of different kinds of marble, with their names; a heap of fruit from different countries" (*VE,* 296b,c). Terms like "pile" and "heap" indicate how haphazard the classification and cataloging must have been. Despite the amateurish display, however, these *cabinets* did have scientific value and made real contributions to learning. From here Montesquieu moved on to the astronomy room, where he found "there are some very handsome and some very good instruments for stargazing."

A third theme that interested Montesquieu the traveler is the economic reality around him. Throughout his life a successful wine producer and merchant, Montesquieu was a business-minded tourist with a special interest in technology. In his report on the Hartz mines he described their special pumps. In Hanover, one of the fountains in the Herrenhausen gardens produced a 120-foot column of water. Montesquieu devoted a long page to an explanation of their mechanism and added a sketch. In Venice, he inspected a dredge. At Ala in the Tyrol a loom for manufacturing velvet caught his attention. While in Venice, he visited the famous glass factory on the island of Murano.

Montesquieu is not satisfied with just these eye-catching examples. He is also, and perhaps even more, interested in the less visible factors on which a nation's economy turns. Thus, he inquires about the finances of almost every state or city he visits. He wants to know the population, the fertility of the soil and its productivity, the expense of keeping a standing army. He investigates the ruler's revenues and the rates of taxation: "The city dwellers of Augsburg are heavily taxed. Since they have nothing but what lies within the city walls, industry has to pay. So that they almost all pay two percent of their capital, which comes to half their income" (*VE,* 310a). The actual facts that Montesquieu records are less important than the serious effort he is making to discern the economic vitality of the countries he visits.

My fourth category focuses on the social milieu in which Montesquieu traveled and the social elites he constantly met. A member of the aristocracy himself, the baron de La Brède naturally sought out those of his own class and felt totally comfortable with them. Armed with letters of introduction and his own international reputation, he moved in social circles whose members comprised an eighteenth-century *Who's Who*. In Vienna he met Emperor Charles VI and Prince Eugene of Savoy who had fought so successfully with Marlborough in Flanders against Louis XIV. During his six months in Rome he frequented the salon of Cardinal de Polignac, the French emissary and minister plenipotentiary to the Vatican. Montesquieu's entry into the Ambrosino Library in Milan was arranged by Countess Borromeo. The fine chateaux and the splendid gardens that he frequently visited and described were, of course, owned by fellow aristocrats. Beginning a paragraph with the phrase "The principal individuals I knew in Vienna," Montesquieu does not hesitate to drop an impressive list of names along with a short indication of each one's pedigree: "Prince Eugene . . . Maréchal Starhemberg . . . Count Kinsky . . . Count Collalto . . . Prince Beveren . . . Count d'Harrach . . . Count Windischgraetz . . . Count Wurmbrand . . . Count Martinitz . . . Prince Lobkowitz, Prince Schwarzenberg, Prince Lichtenstein, Count Zinzendorf . . . Prince La Tour . . . Count Paar" (*VE,* 212c,d). Lest we think that Montesquieu is but a social butterfly, we should notice that he is capable of less flattering judgments about these same individuals: "Pisani, who has 100,000 florins a year income, was a noble ambassador in France; he wants to imitate along the Brenta [river] the gardens of our royal houses. However, he is a rich citizen but a poor prince" (*VE,* 217d).

Montesquieu's journals record the table talk, the idle chatter, and the gossip that he overheard as these powerful individuals talked politics. Representing France in Rome and thus the leading citizen of the French community there, Cardinal de Polignac, a born politician, was deeply involved in all the intrigues of a city that was filled with machinations. Polignac shared with Montesquieu anecdotes about the naïveté of James Francis Edward Stuart, the son of King James II of England who had been deposed by the Glorious Revolution of 1688. Living in exile in Rome, James was called the Old Pretender to distinguish him from his son, Bonnie Prince Charlie, the Young Pretender, who became the stuff of so much history and legend. According to Polignac, the Old Pretender was oblivious to the political maneuvering of those friends and advisers who surrounded him, even though their bickering prevented him from making any serious attempt to regain his throne. Polignac also entertained Montesquieu with inside information about the backroom politicking in the conclave that elected Pope Innocent XIII (*VE,* 286). From shards of conversations Montesquieu partially reconstructs the *Unigenitus* affair that had so bitterly divided France in 1713 by pitting Jesuits against Jansenists. He also collects echoes about the resistance to that papal bull by the Jansenist Cardinal Noailles which was still continuing almost 15 years after the dispute first broke out.

As gossip caught on the fly in various circumstances and situations, these anecdotes are invariably incomplete and often require extensive background information just so today's reader can understand what is at stake. The publication of the papal bull *Unigenitus* during the last years of Louis XIV's reign set the hard-line, conservative Jansenists at loggerheads with the liberal Jesuits who favored a more relaxed doctrine of religious observance and morality. The king and the pope both opposed the Jansenists, who nonetheless maintained strong support among traditionalists, aristocrats, and parliamentary officials. The uproar surrounding the bull mixed into the religious controversy political questions of national sovereignty and patriotic resentment against foreign meddling in domestic affairs. This same quarrel, in multiple variations and spin-offs confronting Jansenist and Jesuit, Gallican and Ultramontane, would polarize religion and politics in France for the rest of the century. Montesquieu's fragmentary record of such conversations again demonstrates his relaxed attitude toward composition. He is writing very much for himself and not for some other, less-informed reader. He does not require a cumbersome critical apparatus to explain the historical and political allusions he himself understood perfectly well. On the contrary, he is trying to capture the light wit and the allusive tone that characterize so much of the eighteenth-century conversational style.

My fifth and final category is a miscellany containing several long-standing interests that deserve comment. Forever seeking the "laws" that uncover unity in apparent diversity, Montesquieu attempts to capture the distinctive national character of the various peoples he meets. He finds the Neapolitans, for example, superstitious, duplicitous, and lacking in taste. More than merely colorful description or facile stereotyping, these terms are intended as defining features that set the Neapolitans apart from others. Montesquieu's search for national or regional characteristics is connected to his considerations on geography and climate. "The Italian likes his comforts more than the Frenchman and is softer. Similarly, the German is tougher than the Frenchman. It appears to me, then, that, the more one moves to the north, the more people are hardened to pain; and the more you go to the south and to warm climates, the more the body is soft and the will weakened" (*VE*, 271a). Although they are admittedly limited, Montesquieu's personal experiences constitute the basis for these large generalizations. An observer and an empiricist, he is constantly looking at specific details in order to discover the larger laws hidden behind them. He writes, for example, that "The Bavarians are more stupid than the Germans. Really, the reaction of the mind in these nations is not instantaneous. It takes a lot of time for their brain to register anything. Whatever order you give, you see them thinking for a long time just to get it into their head, as if you were presenting a geometry problem, and finally they understand you" (*VE*, 311b,c).

His comments on the Dutch seem at first just anecdotal and not that untypical of any tourist in a foreign land: "All that I was told about the avarice, the knavery, the swindling of the Dutch is not at all embellished, it's the pure truth" (*VE*, 327b). Behind such visible behavior, however, he is seeking the deeper explanations for what he has seen: "The heart of those who inhabit countries that live off commerce is entirely corrupted: they never perform the least service for you because they hope that you will buy it from them. Furthermore, Holland is full of ridiculous taxes" (*VE*, 327b). Here Montesquieu connects a nation's mores and its business ethic, a link he will treat at greater length and with more subtlety later in the *Laws*. His judgment on the English is similar in that he again has recourse to business in order to explain national character. Montesquieu discovers "a flaw that seems to me to be that of the genius of the nation . . . which is less preoccupied with its own prosperity than with its jealousy of others' prosperity. That is its dominant spirit as all the laws of England on commerce and navigation show" (*VE*, 334a). Another anecdote illustrates how in Montesquieu's mind everything is intertwined in a web of interdependencies, even though we might find the particular example more suited to England than to Holland: "tea is ruining the Dutch bourgeoisie. A woman drinks thirty cups of tea in the morning. With that, the whole family gets together; a lot of sugar is consumed; the husband hangs around for two hours and wastes his time. Same thing with the servants. Tea weakens women's muscle tone; as a remedy, a number of them take up strong spirits" (*VE*, 327c). Montesquieu can read a nation's destiny in a tea cup: excessive leisure drives out the discipline of hard work, extravagant habits deplete one's wealth uselessly, and an unhealthy diet leads to physical disorders.

To conclude, let me evoke a humbler Montesquieu. Enriched by the new knowledge acquired in his travels, he still retains many of his older habits and beliefs: "Men are incredibly foolish! I feel that I am more attached to my religion now that I have seen Rome and the artistic masterpieces that are in its churches. I am like those leaders of Sparta who did not want Athens to perish because she had produced Sophocles and Euripides and was the mother of so many brilliant men" (*VE*, 328a). Even as he recognizes his own cultural and religious relativism, he nonetheless reaches out for a universalizing, classical comparison. But the most impressive part of his sober and unfanatical support of religion is the opening sentence. Who are these foolish men? Doubtless Montesquieu means to include himself among them. That single touch of self-deprecation captures a good part of Montesquieu's very modern appeal as an inquisitive traveler and a thinking tourist.

Chapter Four

Considerations on the Causes of the Greatness of the Romans and their Decadence

After finishing his long trip through Europe, Montesquieu returned to Bordeaux in 1731 and immediately plunged into reading and research about Rome. While his preparation was serious and thorough, and included reading all the major historians both classical and modern, Montesquieu was able to complete his historical study of Rome in less than three years. *Les Considérations sur les causes de la grandeur des Romains et de leur décadence (Considerations on the Causes of the Greatness of the Romans and their Decadence)* was published in 1734 in Amsterdam by Jean Desbordes. According to some critics, this work was originally conceived as only a single chapter in *The Spirit of the Laws,* but the text grew to such an extent that it had to be published as a separate work. This somewhat uncertain origin would explain certain flaws in the text's overall organization, a topic I will discuss later in this chapter.

Unlike *The Persian Letters,* this book was not a best-seller. Critics were divided as to its merits. Readers in England and Germany were much more positive than the French who did not fathom Montesquieu's intentions. They regretted not finding the frivolity they had enjoyed in *The Persian Letters.* Always jealous of potential rivals and hostile to any contemporary who could make a claim to equal status with him, Voltaire found Montesquieu, like Rome, in decline.

It is difficult for us to appreciate the *Considerations* for a number of reasons. First, we must remember that Montesquieu's educated eighteenth-century readers were much more familiar with Roman history than we are today. Studied in the original texts of Tacitus, Livy, and Sallust, the story of Rome was a major part of their school curriculum. Montesquieu expected that anyone reading his *Considerations* would already have a thorough background in Latin history and literature.

Therefore he could omit what we consider essential information because he assumed it was common knowledge. His Rome is a sophisticated construct that requires considerable background on the part of the reader.

Second, our conception of Rome has been shaped by 200 years of history written since Montesquieu's effort, during which time he has been to a large extent the victim of his own success. His analysis of Rome has become in large part fundamental to all subsequent historians. Although he was one of the first to seek the impact of values and attitudes upon events, Montesquieu's pioneering steps have been largely obliterated by those who have followed along the same path. To cite just one example, Edward Gibbon's *The Decline and Fall of the Roman Empire* (1776–88), *the* history of Rome for the English-speaking world and a classic of eighteenth-century history and literature, has thrown its long shadow over Montesquieu's earlier and much less extensive effort.

In order to get a sense of what Montesquieu was attempting in his history of Rome, I will look briefly at three contemporary or near-contemporary French historians whose work provides an intellectual and methodological context for Montesquieu's. Then I will discuss the structure of the *Considerations.* Finally, I will examine in some detail a few of its principal themes.

Other Historians

In order to understand the *Considerations,* we must keep firmly in mind what Montesquieu was attempting to do. Today, disciplines like sociology, anthropology, and political science all touch on what Montesquieu studied in the Roman empire. However, in the eighteenth century "history" was the only word that covered such a wide area. Obviously, history then could not mean exactly what it does today. For example, in Montesquieu's time narrative history, which is how history was practiced in the late nineteenth and early twentieth century, did not yet exist: it was still waiting to be invented. History was only beginning to take on definitive form as various writers struggled to create what we recognize now as "history writing."

Jacques-Bénigne Bossuet (1627–1704), bishop of Meaux and the leading churchman in France, put theology into the service of history. His *Discours sur l'histoire universelle* (*Discourse on Universal History,* 1681),

written for the Dauphin and intended to educate a future king, records
the impact of divine providence upon human affairs. Whatever happens
is part of God's will. Events that men do not understand nonetheless
belong in God's plan for humanity. If this idea no longer passes muster
as a valid notion of historical process, it remains a good lesson in humility for an all-powerful, absolute monarch: "But remember, Monsieur, that this long chain of individual causes, which make and
unmake empires, depends on the secret orders of Divine Providence. In
his highest heaven God holds the reins of all kingdoms; he holds every
heart in his hand."[1] Bossuet provides a continuous and coherent narrative highlighting kings and wars because "religion and political government are the two points on which all human events turn" (*Discourse,*
40). He divides his *Discourse* into three parts. The first selects 12 epochs, mostly from biblical or Roman history, as the critical facts one
must know in order to understand "universal" history. The second part
retells the story of Israel, the chosen people, and the early church. The
third part, entitled "Empires," studies Greece and Rome.

Despite the limitations of Bossuet's enterprise, a number of his
analyses of the Roman empire resemble Montesquieu's. He sees the
same qualities in the Roman people: "Of all the peoples in the world,
the proudest and the toughest, but all in all the most disciplined in its
deliberations, the most constant in its principles, the most clever, the
most hard-working, and finally the most patient were the Roman people" (*Discourse,* 393). Like Montesquieu, he emphasizes the importance
of military discipline. He understands that while poor and frugal as
individuals, the Romans collectively took pride in erecting costly monuments as a public expression of their national values and achievements.
He points out "the steadfastness of the senate in the midst of so many
reverses" (*Discourse,* 405) and its "profound politics" (*Discourse,* 400)
whose secret intentions were never betrayed. Montesquieu would be
more critical of the devious nature of this impenetrable senate. Like
Montesquieu, Bossuet offers a long parallel comparing and contrasting
Carthage and Rome. He, too, looks beyond surfaces in order to uncover
the hidden motivations of peoples and nations:

Nature does not fail to produce in all countries outstanding intelligence and
courage, but she has to be helped in forming them. What forms them, what
perfects them, are the strong sentiments and the noble impressions that are
spread among all individuals and that pass unnoticed from one to another.
What makes our nobility so proud in combat and so aggressive in its under-

takings? It is a notion inculcated from childhood and reinforced by the unanimous feeling of the nation, that a gentleman without heart disgraces himself and is no longer worthy to see the light of day. All Romans were brought up with this feeling, and the people vied with the nobility to see who would adhere most to these vigorous principles. (*Discourse,* 404–5)

It is only in passing, however, that Bossuet succeeds in revealing the secret attitudes and the hidden causes that Montesquieu will make the main thrust of his analysis.

Pierre Bayle (1647–1706) wrote the *Dictionnaire historique et critique* (*Historical and Critical Dictionary,* 1697) that remained an influential book especially among *philosophes* throughout the eighteenth century. A militant Protestant persecuted by the Catholic church, Bayle had a secret agenda in writing his history. He wanted to demonstrate the power of human reason and at the same time to unmask the falsehoods encouraged by religion. In his *Dictionary,* Bayle relentlessly pursued historical error with skeptical detachment. He compiled the facts and, more important, the fictions surrounding great figures like the biblical David. Then his corrosive intelligence separated the wheat from the chaff. In a sense, he wrote negative history, demonstrating how false supposedly true accounts of "facts" can be. Bayle wanted to show how little we really know and how certain institutions have compounded our ignorance.

Despite its immense erudition, Bayle's *Dictionary* has no center. He arranged it alphabetically so each entry would be self-contained. A compilation of discrete bits, the whole never becomes a sequential history, nor does it provide a coherent picture of the past. Due to its size and the mass of scholarship it displays, Bayle's achievement is impressive, but we would not easily recognize it as history writing today.

Of all the French historians of this period, the most famous is Voltaire. While Montesquieu was writing the *Considerations,* Voltaire published his *Histoire de Charles XII, Roi de Suède* (*History of Charles XII, King of Sweden,* 1731), which was organized around the single figure mentioned in the title who dominated all the action of the story. His *Le Siècle de Louis XIV* (*Century of Louis XIV,* 1751) marks the limits of this "great man" theory of history. As monarch Louis did personify his times, but even as Voltaire consecrates this identification of the man and his epoch, he begins to recognize the impact of institutions and collective mind-sets. In his final chapters he gives them their due. Finally, his *Essai sur les moeurs et l'esprit des nations* (Essay on mores,

1756/1761) attempts to present the history of society and culture as a collective, cooperative phenomenon beyond the shaping of any single individual. Although the similarity with Montesquieu is evident just from the title, Voltaire never fails to produce a comprehensible and continuous narrative of events. While seeking out the whys beneath the surface of historical events, he is most concerned with providing a fact-filled narrative securely kept in place with names and dates. A recent critic has emphasized Voltaire's contribution to the making of modern history writing. According to Patrick Henry, Voltaire "replaced the purely chronological approach to historiography by the analytical and moved the writing of history from the chronicles of battles to the history of society and the progress of mankind."[2] Without denying Voltaire his due, I would still maintain that Montesquieu preceded him in abandoning mere chronicle and in embracing critical analysis.

In writing the *Considerations,* Montesquieu was not interested in finding the hand of God in the affairs of men, nor did he envision history as a vast compendium of facts with little or no causal relations among them. Nor did he believe that a single individual, no matter how extraordinary, could completely determine the flow of history: history is not just the biography of kings and generals. On the contrary, he attempted to provide an alternative historiography, one that had not existed before and therefore one that he would have to invent. His *Considerations* is an early and bold attempt at analytic history writing. It seeks out invisible principles and deep causes behind the events that its readers already knew quite well. What Montesquieu is studying lies below the visible surface of events. "What" has a near tangible reality; "why" belongs entirely to the abstract realm. What makes reading this book difficult is precisely what makes it original. Montesquieu's history marks the attempt to discover invisible causes and to locate the motor of history inside the spirit and the attitudes of a people as a mass, of a nation as a whole.

Structure

Any attempt to summarize the historical facts in the *Considerations* would be an exercise in futility. We can, however, profitably attempt to understand the structure of the book and to seize how Montesquieu organized these facts. Armed with such an overview and the interpretation such an overview implies, readers can explore the details of the text on their own.

One outline was prepared by Montesquieu himself or else by Père Castel, his close friend and adviser.[3] It divides the work into two unequal parts. Books 1 through 8 deal with the rise of Rome, books 9 to 23 with her decadence or decline. The subheadings do not refer to specific chapters, but rather to the major explanations that Montesquieu offers for either the rise or fall of Rome.

Greatness of the Romans: Causes of Their Growth (1–8)

1. Triumphal entries and ceremonies
2. Adoption of foreign customs that they judged superior to their own
3. Their laws
4. The consuls' self-interest in behaving as honorable men during their term of office
5. The distribution of booty to soldiers and conquered lands to citizens
6. Continuous warfare
7. Their steadfastness in every trial which kept them from discouragement
8. Their skill in destroying enemies one by one
9. An excellent government which had mechanisms for correcting abuses

Decadence of Roman Greatness: Its Causes (9–23)

1. Wars in faraway countries
2. Giving Roman citizenship to all allies
3. The insufficiency of its laws during the time of its greatness
4. Moral depravity
5. Abolition of triumphal processions
6. Invasion of barbarians into the empire
7. Barbarian soldiers incorporated into the regular Roman armies in too great numbers

While recognizing that this outline succinctly captures the main points of Montesquieu's argument, I would like to propose a different organization that shapes the book in a more effective manner.

I divide the *Considerations* into three parts followed by a long coda. The first part, chapters 1 through 7, describes how the grandeur of Rome was achieved. The seeds of future greatness are traced back to its bellicose origins with Tarquin (1), its military techniques and discipline (2), and its first great victory over Carthage (4). Chapter 3 describes the early Romans as a homogeneous society in which wealth and lands were evenly divided. A high proportion of the population was young and all citizens fulfilled their military duty. With a brief forward look, Montesquieu contrasts this happy civic state with Rome's later corruption (and with eighteenth-century Europe) where avarice and prodigality concentrate wealth in a few hands and where the social extremes of rich and poor eclipse the productive citizen-soldiers in the middle. Although change is dangerous and will eventually spell Rome's doom, at times it is necessary for survival. Early Rome knew how to change successfully and to adopt the best of what it found in its enemies. Because the Greeks (5) failed to modify their phalanxes, the Roman legions defeated them. Hannibal beat the Romans when he adopted their tactics: "What contributed heavily to imperil the Romans in the second Punic war was that Hannibal at first armed his troops like the Romans: but the Greeks changed neither their weapons nor their tactics. It never occurred to them to renounce those habits with which they had accomplished so much."[4]

The Senate (6) offered a model of stability and steadfastness for the Roman character. Without deviating from its decision to act always like masters and never to waiver in any decision, it consistently divided its enemies and weakened its allies. It never made peace in good faith and was not above abusing the language of its treaties if Rome could find some profit therein: "These Roman customs were not specific or isolated facts that happened by chance; they were principles steadfastly maintained" (*Considerations*, 447d). Mithradates (7) resisted Rome so long and successfully because he possessed many of the same virtues and advantages that the early Romans themselves did. When Pompey finally defeated him, that victory marked both the high point of Rome's empire and the first step on the path to decadence and decline: "It was then that Pompey, by the speed of his victories, completed the pompous work of Rome's greatness. He brought vast expanses into the empire which served more for the spectacle of Roman magnificence than for its true power. And, although the banners carried in his triumphal entry proclaimed that he had augmented the treasury by more than a third, Rome's power did not increase and liberty was only further exposed" (*Considerations*, 450). For Montesquieu, this high watermark of the Roman empire provides the dramatic and logical ending for his consideration of Rome's greatness. Rome teeters on the precarious edge of its greatest victory and largest territorial expansion. Just on the other side of this success begins the inevitable decline.

In the next three chapters Montesquieu scrutinizes this critical *moment* of transition from grandeur to decadence which his title announced so emphatically. I place the word *moment* in italics since this transition is not easily localized in any specific temporal dimension. Montesquieu has not given us a chronological narrative. Instead, he is interested in the interior life of Roman culture. He pursues not a sequential unfolding of events in time, but rather a vertical analysis of mental or moral phenomena within their larger social context. Let me illustrate the distinction with examples taken from Père Castel's outline cited earlier. When did the "excellent government" fall into the "insufficiency of its laws during the period of its greatness"? How to explain the difference between successful "continuous warfare" and debilitating "wars in faraway countries"? In these three central chapters Montesquieu locates the perilous passage from one mental, political, and moral state to another.

Chapter 8 is entitled "Divisions that Always Existed in the City." Here as elsewhere Montesquieu does not date his facts since he is dealing more with attitudes and perceptions than with precise, historical events. Such attitudes would in any case be extremely difficult to pinpoint chronologically since they are ongoing experiences that only become critical under certain circumstances. From primitive Rome through the Republic an intense rivalry divided patricians and plebeians. For a long period this conflict produced only a healthy tension, an energy that could be directed outward and into productive enterprises like foreign wars. But this dynamic balance could not last forever. Once the equipoise was ruptured, each side strove to dominate the other rather than to reinstate the shattered equilibrium.

Chapter 9 deals with two factors that caused the loss of Roman identity and hence of national character. First, the soldier forgot that he was first and foremost a citizen and began to feel a greater loyalty to his general than to his country: "They were no longer the soldiers of the Republic, but rather the soldiers of Sylla, Marius, Pompey, or Caesar" (*Considerations,* 452c). Coupled with the increasing number of foreign recruits and the wars fought further from the center of the nation, which was the city of Rome itself, this change radically affected the discipline of the army upon whose success in war the entire empire was based.

Second, as more foreigners were granted Roman citizenship, the concept of being a Roman lost its unifying power. This right was no longer as exclusive as it once had been. Opening the rolls of citizenship also opened the original Roman character to the risk of dilution by mixing it with other racial stocks. Although we in America today see the "melting-pot" concept as an integral part of our national strength,

Montesquieu thought that the Roman spirit and its special genius were weakened by foreigners who did not always share the same background and the same values: "Then Rome was no longer that city whose people had only one spirit, one love for liberty, and one hatred for tyranny. . . . When the peoples of Italy became her citizens, each city brought its own genius, its own special interests. . . . The city was torn and no longer made a single whole" (*Considerations*, 453a). Unable to remain true to her original nature, Rome was equally unable to duplicate her original successes.

Chapter 10 focuses on moral corruption. Epicureanism, the hedonistic philosophy imported from the East, destroyed the "heart and the spirit of the Romans" because it undermined the bellicose character and the strict military discipline of earlier times. Epicurius's philosophy softened the rough and calloused hands of the conquering legions and thus, indirectly, defeated them. As Montesquieu had already suggested in his paradoxical assessment of Pompey's victory over Mithradates, Rome was weakened by her very victories because they brought back enormous quantities of booty. The spoils of war introduced luxury but not prosperity into the economy. As a consequence of this unprecedented wealth that they did not have to work to earn, the Romans lost their motivation and eventually their talent for business and for the arts. Rather than engage in trade or craftsmanship themselves, they came to despise those skills and abandoned them to their slaves.

Incredibly successful as a small city-state, Rome crumbled under its own weight once it became a powerful and far-flung empire. Always for Montesquieu the profound causes are not specific personalities or battles but rather the nature of the people, their attitudes and customs, and their particular genius: "good laws, which allowed a small republic to become large, impose a burden once it has grown. . . . Rome lost her liberty because she completed her work too soon" (*Considerations*, 453d).

The third part of the *Considerations,* chapters 11 through 20, goes over more familiar territory and therefore is much easier to follow as an historical narrative. Chapters 11 through 16, all with emperors' names in their titles, offer a somewhat more traditional story line of events set in a clearer chronological frame. Battles and the struggle for power fill chapter 11. Caesar (11 and 12) perfected some of the old Roman virtues while corrupting others. After the long period of civil war, Augustus (13) reestablished a temporary equilibrium. Although many consider Augustus's reign to be one of the glories of the Roman legacy, Montesquieu is much more suspicious of this near-absolute ruler who dominated his time much as Louis XIV did his: "Sylla, a temperamental man, leads the Romans violently to liberty; Augustus, the crafty tyrant, leads them softly to slavery" (*Considerations*, 461a).

The full weight of the accumulating moral changes can be felt in chapters 14–16 which rehearse the empire's long disintegration under Tiberius, Caligula, Nero, and a series of gradually weaker emperors. Only briefly does Marcus Aurelius brighten the picture because he is true to the old values and attempts to restore them, albeit unsuccessfully. Once begun, Rome's slide is inevitable and unstoppable.

The last two chapters offer general summaries of this national decadence and decline. In chapter 17 Montesquieu details the "Change in the State." He notes the impact of moral softness and a loss of the warlike spirit. By the time the empire was divided in two, the taste for Asiatic pomp and splendor had completely triumphed over the original Roman frugality: "when Julien attempted to put some simplicity and modesty in his manner, what was only the memory of former mores was now called forgetting dignity" (*Considerations*, 470a). Chapter 18 lists the new attitudes that characterized the empire and that contrast with those of early Rome mentioned in chapters 2 and 6. One maxim summarizes the factor that Montesquieu sees as the root cause of Rome's fate: "Thus they established customs that were entirely contrary to those that had made them masters of the world" (*Considerations*, 472a). Change is dangerous when it alters the basic character of a nation and contradicts the principles of its original success.

It is only at this point, late in his study, that Montesquieu articulates the basic methodology that has been guiding him throughout his analysis of Rome: "It is not fortune or luck that rules the world. . . . There are general causes, either moral or physical, that are at work in each monarchy, that raise it up, sustain it, or knock it down. All that happens is subject to these causes; . . . in a word, the principal characteristic drags along with it all the accidental particulars" (*Considerations*, 472c). Nearly hidden in the middle of the chapter, this paragraph is a short and modest declaration of a revolutionary new way of writing history. Montesquieu will spend the next 20 years perfecting this insight as he works on his masterpiece, *The Spirit of the Laws*, which illustrates the principle of underlying causes and crowns his attempt to approach such topics analytically and not anecdotally. Ironically, the unaccented position of this critical statement only serves to highlight the absence of any preface, introduction, or similar explanation of purpose or method at the beginning of the book. This lapse in planning and shaping the entire work justifies treating the last chapters as an afterthought, what I call the coda.

The final group of chapters, 21–23, which deal with the Eastern Empire after the Fall of Rome, add nothing new to Montesquieu's analysis. In fact, they look very much out of place. Chapter 22, for example, examines Christianity's negative impact on the empire. Up to this point Montesquieu has avoided the dangerous subject of religion. Nonetheless, had he really intended to discuss Christianity's impact, it would have been more logical to place that discussion in the chapters on Rome than in those on Constantinople.

Because these final chapters appear to be an afterthought that prolongs the book beyond its proper range, I characterize them as a coda, an appendage related to the main body but not really an integral part of it. This interpretation is not farfetched since most critics consider the *Considerations* a rehearsal for *The Spirit of the Laws* which itself has a few unlikely chapters tacked on at its end. I have already stated that initially the *Considerations* was planned as a chapter in the *Laws*. Given that origin as a piece of some greater whole, it is easier to understand that Montesquieu would be more concerned with finding material and developing arguments than with perfecting their presentation. He could leave this history of Rome a bit untidy and unfinished because he intended to return to much of this same material at a later date.

Considering the final three chapters as a coda allows for a more coherent structure for the whole. The seven chapters of the first part balance more evenly the ten chapters in the third. In the middle, Montesquieu's effort at understanding history pivot on the three chapters that analyze the precarious and perilous moment of transition.

Principal Themes

The *Considerations* is not a book without failings. As we have just seen, it ends fitfully. Throughout, it provides only a weak narrative and a tenuous chronology. Montesquieu is mainly interested in discussing attitudes and customs, and these he rarely if ever dates. He does not indicate when citizens stopped being soldiers, for example, nor when military discipline entered its decline. Neither does he indicate the steps in the progression from one widely accepted attitude or *esprit* to another. He draws examples from various times to illustrate a single point. He never clearly distinguishes the various epochs of Rome's government because he assumed that his readers had the background to fill all this in for themselves. Despite such shortcomings (and it could be argued that they are shortcomings not of the book but of its readers), this history of Rome illustrates two important points about Montesquieu the writer: his typically eighteenth-century fondness for one particular metaphor and his highly polished, lapidary style.

One of the most prominent metaphors in eighteenth-century thinking and one that Montesquieu uses extensively is mechanical.[5] In politics, the state is a machine that is activated by weights and counterweights just as, for deists, God is the great clockmaker who, having created the universe as an admirable assembly of springs and levers, allows the mechanism to run on its own. It is perhaps not off the point to mention that the eighteenth century produced many accurate, operational models of the solar system and of how it functioned. Called orreries after the invention's sponsor, Charles Boyle, earl of Orrery, they were essentially large clocklike machines that positioned the planets in their orbits and regulated all their interdependent movements with rods and springs. Like religion and politics, science and history embraced this mechanical metaphor.

What is important to note here is that the metaphor is counterbalanced and symmetrical. This same feeling is present in Montesquieu's title: "greatness" and "decadence," the two symmetrical swings of the same movement, up and down, rise and fall, weight and counterweight. In the hands of Montesquieu this machine metaphor becomes a powerful tool for understanding the variety and the apparent unpredictability of human activity.

Montesquieu writes as if he intends, like the orreries, to illustrate the mechanical metaphor in action. Critics have often considered his style an attempt to create striking phrases called *formules* or *maximes* in French. I would argue that, on the contrary, Montesquieu's thinking is accurately reflected in his favorite rhetorical patterns. The compact equations that he writes are "formulae" in both the rhetorical and mathematical senses. As rhetoric, his sentences baffle criticism. Their lapidary expression cannot be easily broken down into separate components. By avoiding such dissection, they escape from the analytic scrutiny that disassembles whole arguments piece by piece and refutes each in turn. Unmovable and unyielding, these tightly knit sentences thwart the reader's skepticism and foil any attempt to disagree. Concise and compact, they produce an effect beyond their simple meaning. Their stylistic self-assurance carries as it were a guarantee of their ideological validity. I might go so far as to say that Montesquieu's style replicates

the process of his study. Searching for the deep-seated laws that govern
our behavior even when we are not consciously aware of them, Montesquieu puts into his phrases a sense of those laws in operation. Imper-
sonal forces just beyond the horizon of our perception, these mechanical
operations of action and reaction, of cause and effect, filter down into
the words that are being used to describe them.

To complete my discussion of the *Considerations,* I would like to
examine now a few of its principle themes. Since I am treating Montesquieu's works in chronological order, I will take the opportunity to
look back to similar ideas in *The Persian Letters* and anticipate their
reformulation in *The Spirit of the Laws.*

The first such focal point is the importance of national character. For
Montesquieu there is a definable spirit in each nation or people that
distinguishes them from any other. Every people possesses a particular
genius that explains how, or rather why, they behave the way they do.
Consequently, he devotes a good deal of effort to uncovering the spirit
of the Romans. It becomes most apparent in the contrast of Rome with
Carthage: "In Rome, governed by laws, the people allowed the Senate
to undertake the direction of their public affairs; in Carthage, governed
by abuse [of laws], the people wanted to do everything for themselves"
(*Considerations,* 441b). The sentences are so symmetrical in syntax and
word order that the change of the single term "laws" to "abuse" stands
out while the two clauses, although divergent in meaning, mirror each
other closely in the original French. The echo in *affaires* and *faire* ("human affairs" and "to do") is lost in translation, as is the repetition of
the verb endings ("souff*rait*" and "voul*ait*") which is much stronger
than the English "allow*ed*" and "want*ed.*" Here the rhetorical device of
the parallel is exploited to its full extent. Slight differences are magni-
fied while the basic similarities are maintained, the shift in a single
word producing an emphatic result. Without resorting to any excessive means, Montesquieu quietly but effectively rivets our attention on
the key words and concepts.

Again playing on the symmetry of vocabulary and syntax, Montesquieu pictures the struggle between these two cities as a battle of moral
values, envisioned as degrading opulence versus ennobling poverty.
Carthage's negative and external wealth, defined by two lifeless metals,
is swamped by Rome's four positive moral qualities. "Carthage, which
made war with its opulence against Rome's poverty, found a disadvan-
tage in that very fact. Gold and silver can be used up; but virtue,
steadfastness, strength, and poverty never can be" (*Considerations,*

441b). For idiomatic reasons my translation unfortunately does not repeat the strong term "use up" as Montesquieu does. His single verb "s'épuiser" plays on two registers of meaning, one moral, the other physical. Montesquieu chooses not to discuss logistics or military tactics. He does not invoke the war's other causes, that is, economic and imperialistic rivalries. He sees national character as the fundamental, tangible reality, and not as some abstraction. Attitude, character, spirit belong to Montesquieu's vocabulary of viable causal factors, just as economic or military superiority might belong to someone else's.

In addition to questions of character, Montesquieu is fascinated by the relationship of any nation to its ruling process and to its laws. For him the ideal state is comprised of active members, citizens who participate willingly and knowingly in their own governance. "There is nothing so powerful as a republic in which laws are observed not out of fear, not by reason, but by passion as they were in Sparta and Rome. For then to the wisdom of a good government is joined all the strength that a faction could have" (*Considerations,* 441b). We remember the good Troglodytes who possessed such civic virtue and therefore lived in a utopia. Over and over Montesquieu reiterates the critical importance for any state of laws that are clearly enunciated, that govern all the people, and that the citizens observe voluntarily.

As was the case with the Troglodytes, written and official laws are not sufficient. Laws must live in the hearts and in the practice of the citizens. Hence for Montesquieu the Roman censors fulfilled an essential function. They did not just count the population but they maintained the civic passion just mentioned: "since the strength of the republic consisted in its discipline, the austerity of its mores, and the continuous observance of certain customs, [the censors] corrected those abuses that the law had not foreseen or that the ordinary judges could not punish" (*Considerations,* 451c). Montesquieu always emphasizes this delicate and nearly undefinable balance between the letter and the spirit of the law. Here he is a philosopher and not at all a lawyer since the latter instinctively rebel at any preference for the living spirit over the written letter of the law. Montesquieu understands that no written code can cover all eventualities and that laws are meaningless unless they are fairly implemented in differing circumstances. Knowing these difficulties, he concurs with the (to legalistic eyes, dangerous) notion that "the assassin of whoever usurped sovereign power" would be "a virtuous man" (*Considerations,* 457). Citizens are active members of their republic, ready to assume the awesome responsibility of acting outside the usual laws in order to obey a higher law. Today more than in the eighteenth century too many possibilities for anarchism and vigilante justice exist in such behavior. In Montesquieu's mind, any potential for abuse would be obviated by the civic virtue and passion that would bind all the citizens together and prevent individual excess.

If Rome's rise can be found in its moral character, so, too, can its fall. Rome's fate is a product of its special genius and bears the same marks as its rise: "That fearful tyranny of the emperors came from the general spirit of the Romans. As they fell suddenly under an arbitrary government and as there was hardly any distinction among them between ordering and obeying, they were not prepared for this change by gentler mores: their temperament remained ferocious. Citizens were treated as they themselves had treated their conquered enemies and they were ruled in similar fashion" (*Considerations*, 463d). Here the inevitable circle completes its full revolution. Earlier Montesquieu commented that never was there a "better slave" nor a "meaner master" than Caligula: "For these two things are quite related" (*Considerations*, 463c). The eunuchs in Usbek's harem illustrate the same truth as the decadent Romans do. Slaves are not active citizens who participate in ruling the state. Consequently, they never learn how to govern either themselves or others: "the same bent of mind that produces a man who is quite impressed by the unlimited power of another who commands also produces a man who is not less impressed when he comes to command himself" (*Considerations*, 463c).

Stability and change are critical elements in Montesquieu's view of national character. Rome's strength was the constancy of the Senate and its ability to act slowly but decisively according to a plan that, once fixed, brooked no deviation: "in the course of so much prosperity, when usually one lets go a bit, the Senate continued to act always with the same profundity" (*Considerations*, 446c). Any activity can endanger the state when the conditions that originally inspired and justified that behavior change: "But the distinctions that were necessary in a republic in order to maintain that government could be nothing but fatal to government under the emperors" (*Considerations*, 477c). The social divisions between patricians and plebeians were arbitrated by the Senate and the censors who channeled the energy and the character of the Roman people in worthwhile directions. Although most social conflicts were successfully harnessed, the resulting equilibrium was always precarious. Once the republican apparatus of counterweights balancing such tensions no longer existed, the rule of the emperors became uncompensated change, change out of control, facile change based on the whim of an individual and not on the deliberation of a collective body reflecting shared attitudes.

Montesquieu is also interested in the impact of the outside, physical world on the inner, mental man. Physical factors such as size and climate will loom large in *The Spirit of the Laws*. Here Montesquieu does not develop these themes at great length although they are present. He does point out how the successful expansion of the empire through its military conquests did eventually overextend the government and undermine it. By extending citizenship to more and more conquered peoples, Rome also increased its size (its number of citizens) and thus diluted its original and particularly Roman character.

In stark contrast to the usual mechanical metaphors, a rarely used natural image is worth mentioning. In discussing the social divisions that kept the factions of patricians and plebeians in conflict, Montesquieu compares them to a volcano: "While Rome was conquering the universe, there was a secret war taking place within its walls. It was a fire like those of a volcano which belch forth as soon as some matter increases its fermentation" (*Considerations*, 450c). Compared at first to those of war, the flames of the volcano are insidious and hidden, doing their work of destruction in secret. The volcano finally explodes when some additional combustible matter is added. This metaphor accurately describes one key aspect of Montesquieu's own historical method. Beneath the visible surface of historical phenomena, deep causes are silently at work. Only when they explode does their long preparation and period of incubation become evident. I have already mentioned how Montesquieu fails to give either a traditional chronology or a sense of various social phenomena coexisting as rivals. The volcano analogy helps to explain this. Like the volcano's fires, the loss of military discipline, for example, was drawn out over centuries. Unnoticed, it does not enter Montesquieu's analysis until it has reached the bursting point. Physical explosion, like moral change, deserves discussion only when it happens. History cannot be the compendium of might-have-beens. Still, that sudden and spectacular explosion should not obscure the long invisible fermentation even if the former is easier to recognize than the latter. On the contrary, that unexpected explosion offers the most convincing and exciting proof that deep-seated causes were indeed at work.

The *Considerations* is a curious and provocative work. Largely forgotten today, it nonetheless represents an important step in the creation of modern historical writing. It is an acute analysis of the Roman empire to which all subsequent historians of Rome are indebted. It is the embodiment in the historical mode of those ideas on government that Montesquieu had already advanced in the fiction of *The Persian Letters* and that he will later develop in the anthropological and sociological arguments of *The Spirit of the Laws*. Finally, it is a meditation on living, a lesson on how peoples and nations rise through mighty efforts and fall in comfort. Despite its flaws, the *Considerations* is a text that has much to teach our modern times.

Chapter Five
The Spirit of the Laws

Outline

It is very difficult to provide an analytic outline of *De l'Esprit des lois* (*The Spirit of the Laws*) or a summary of the material in it. This immense work does not lend itself to simplification. Montesquieu has treated so many subjects in such detail that the reader can quite easily get lost among the trees and not see the forest. Compounding the difficulty, some chapters are lengthy and filled with (what seems to us today) arcane material while others are but a few lines long.

To get at the underlying structure of the *Laws,* I propose an outline that will not repeat Montesquieu's highly redundant chapter titles. Furthermore, my entries are arranged both typographically and grammatically so as to emphasize their interrelations. In his own preface Montesquieu claimed that his underlying plan, obscured by the mass of illustrations and examples, would be more easily apparent in the whole than in the details. Although critics still argue on this count, I do believe that a coherent overall structure for the *Laws* exists. My outline follows the division into six parts that Montesquieu himself approved for the 1750 edition.

First Part

1. Definition of law
2. Three governments: despotism, monarchy, republic
3. Three principles: fear, honor, virtue
4. Forming principles: education
5.   Legislator
6.   Magistrate
7. Maintaining principles: luxury and women
8. Losing principles: corruption

Second Part

9. Defensive wars
10. Offensive wars
11. Liberty and the separation of powers
12. Liberty and citizens
13. Liberty and taxes

Third Part

14. Climate and its influence: theory
15.   Climate and slavery
16.   Climate and domestic servitude: women
17. Climate and its influence: theory
18. Geography and its influence
19. Mores and their influence

In the first edition of 1748, the second and final quarto volume began with the fourth part. Montesquieu was dissuaded from placing here an "Invocation to the Muses" that would have balanced the preface at the very beginning of the whole work. Here then is the very center of the work where it divides into two halves of three parts each.

Fourth Part

20. Commerce in monarchies and republics
21. Commerce as symbol and philosophy
22. Money and economics
23. Population

Fifth Part

24. Religion: internal considerations
25. Religion: external manifestations
26. Different laws, different spheres

Sixth Part

27. Roman laws on inheritance
28.   The Franks' civil law
29. Comparative study of law
30.   The Franks and origins of the French monarchy
31.   The Franks and origins of the French monarchy

This outline attempts to articulate the major thrusts and the organizational patterns of Montesquieu's masterpiece. To comment briefly upon it, working backward, part 6 deals with feudal laws and customs, while part 5 contains a very delicate handling of the potentially explosive issue of religion. Part 4 concentrates on economic factors: trade, money, and population affect how people live and consequently how they are governed. While centered on his theory of climate, part 3 addresses factors both physical (weather and geography) and historical (customs) that impinge upon human behaviors. Part 2 deals with a pair of closely related themes, war and liberty. The arrangement of part 1 is more complex than the others, but it, too, is amenable to a logical organization. After the definition of law (chapter 1), the nature of government (2) stands in parallel to its principles (3). Three chapters on forming, maintaining, and inevitably losing those sustaining principles are interrupted by a discussion of how laws are made (5) and how they are enforced (6).

This outline imposes an organization that is not immediately apparent while reading Montesquieu's text. What speaks in its favor is that it allows us to rise above the minute detail and to get a sense of the whole. For example, part 3 is structured like a chiasmus, sandwiching two related themes (slavery and domestic servitude) between two books that also have close affinities (the theory of climate). My outline therefore permits us to better understand the direction of Montesquieu's arguments and appreciate how he has marshaled them. Since part 6 is usually considered an appendix, I would propose that book 26 is the real conclusion of the *Laws*. It offers a symmetrical counterpart to the dramatic opening of the work. Book 1 proposed a new definition of law while book 26 is equally innovative in distinguishing common law from enacted legislation; local from international laws; and civil from religious laws. These distinctions cap the critical argument that religious and political authority should be separate. More important, however, book 26 shares the same theoretical and abstract concerns as book 1. After opening his work with the radical concept that law is a relationship that changes as a function of its component parts, Montesquieu closes it by reminding us that laws belonging to different spheres must not be mixed indiscriminately.

Once again, I must emphasize that my outline is both real and apparent. Real because it serves to orient us as we read, but apparent because we so easily lose sight of it as we read. The strength and paradoxically the weakness of the *Laws* lie in its details. Montesquieu discusses such a wide variety of cases; he alludes to so many historical episodes that have been totally forgotten by today's readers; he jumps

all over the world in search of supporting evidence so that as a result
we simply lose track of the purposes behind his enormous erudition.

Before beginning a more detailed analysis of each book, let me mention quickly two alternative outlines. A *manuel scolaire* widely used in
France, Lagarde et Michard, divides the *Laws* into three parts with the
first book as a separate introduction.[1] The first part, running from
books 2–13, is called "Political Science." The second, books 14–25, is
given the title "Politics and Geography," while the third part, books
26–31, is called "Politics and the History of Law." In a book designed
for students preparing for the French baccalaureate exams, Jean Lecomte
offers a more elaborate model.[2] Again, book 1 is in a category by itself,
"Principles and Definitions." Although critics always place the opening
book apart, few if any connect it to book 26 or see those two books as
the complementary end points and the theoretical bases of Montesquieu's enterprise. Lecomte's second part (books 2–11) is entitled "The
Connections between Laws and the Nature and Principles of Government." Books 12–19 are grouped as "Connections between Laws and
Citizens," while books 20–23 are called "Connections between Laws
and Economic Conditions." The fifth part, books 24–25, deals with
"Connections between Laws and Religion." The last part, books 26–31,
is simply called "Appendix." There is not much serious disagreement
between these two arrangements although Lecomte's six parts are
widely disproportionate in terms of length. In both these outlines the
same terms reappear and often divisions are made at the same points.
Nonetheless, these outlines do not, in my opinion, give a sufficient
sense of the structure of Montesquieu's work nor a feeling for its dynamic thrust. Their most serious failing is that they do not aid the
readers, overwhelmed by details, to recognize the purpose behind the
waves of scholarship that threaten to drown them.

Let us now examine each of the six sections of the *Laws* in turn. Since
no discussion could do justice to Montesquieu's encyclopedic scope, I
will limit myself to major issues. After having been introduced to the
overarching ideas, readers can explore the details of the text on their
own.

First Part: Books 1–8

The first part of *The Spirit of the Laws* is one of the best-known
sections of Montesquieu's entire work because it contains many of the
ideas for which he is most famous.

Before beginning his examination of the "connections that laws should have with the constitution of every government, [and with its] mores, climate, religion, commerce, etc." (that is the book's subtitle), Montesquieu defines a critical term that he will use throughout the book. "What I call *virtue* in a republic is love of the fatherland, that is to say, the love of equality. It is not a moral virtue, nor a Christian virtue, it is a *political* virtue" ("Avertissement de l'auteur" ["Author's Notice"], p. 227; italics in original).[3] Montesquieu knowingly uses a word full of religious resonance in a decidedly non religious context, replacing its moral connotations with a civic meaning. This dechristianization is at the heart of the *Laws*, as Montesquieu's contemporary critics so readily pointed out. The sword, however, cuts both ways. By insisting on a term that had so many unforgettable implications, Montesquieu also raised the duties of the citizen to a higher moral plane and endowed the mechanical functioning of government with spiritual value. In this same preface Montesquieu defines his methodology: "I have set out my principles and I have seen individual cases fit them naturally; the histories of all nations follow them closely; and each specific law connect to another law or depend on a more general one" ("Author's Notice," p. 229). Although Montesquieu is not always entirely faithful to this credo, as critics have noted, this sentence does underline two key methodological concepts. First, Montesquieu seeks out those abstract and hidden principles that alone explain the immense variety of human behavior. Second, he proceeds *deductively* from these general laws to the specific, historical events, *not inductively*, from the specific, instance to the principle. Later, he insists on the interconnectedness of all the phenomena he discusses: "Here many truths will not be felt until we have seen the chain that links them to others. The more we reflect on the details, the more we will feel the certitude of the principles" ("Author's Notice," 229). Previously hidden, these links become visible only in the light of his investigation.

His enterprise thus grounded, Montesquieu defines law as the "necessary connections that derive from the nature of things" (1:1:232). Every phenomenon, even God, has its laws. Clearly, Montesquieu is not talking about judicial laws alone. His concept of law is much larger and much more modern. He uses the word *law* the way we use it when we speak about the "laws" of physics and chemistry. Constant and invariable, these laws express the relationship among physical phenomena, as in the law of gravity, for example. Montesquieu imagines himself as a natural scientist discovering the laws that explain why men behave as they do: why they developed specific customs, why they founded different governments, and why they have different religions.

Revealing this physics of human history is Montesquieu's aim: "This is what I am undertaking in this work. I will examine all these relationships: taken all together they will form what I call THE SPIRIT OF THE LAWS" (1:3:238; capitals in original). Laws are relationships and their intricate interconnections constitute the essence of the law, or, as the title of his book puts it, *The Spirit of the Laws*.

According to Montesquieu there are three types or basic models of government: "the republican government is one where the people as a body, or even a part of the people, have sovereign power; the monarchical, where a single individual governs, but according to fixed and established laws. In contrast, under despotism, an individual without law or restraint moves everything by his will and caprice" (2:1:239). All historical examples can be reduced to these three types. At this point Montesquieu makes no value judgments. He is interested in how governments function and in how laws work in each different situation. Aware that laws are a question of balance and equilibrium, Montesquieu often formulates his ideas in terms of ratios and proportions, for example, "Under any government, the extent of power must be counterbalanced by its brief duration" (2:3:246). A page later he continues, "the more an aristocracy approaches a democracy, the more perfect it will be; and it will be less perfect to the extent that it approaches a monarchy" (2:3:247).

In Montesquieu's system, republics are of two types: democracy, where all the people rule, and aristocracy (we would say oligarchy), where a single class rules. The democratic republic's essence lies in its citizens' right to govern themselves directly, just as they did in Athens or Sparta; the aristocratic republic's essence consists of the citizens' right to select those who will rule in the name of all, in the manner of Rome and its Senate.

The essence of the monarchy is that the king (Montesquieu uses the term "prince" to indicate the ruler of any government) is limited by "fundamental laws" (2:4:247). These "intermediary, subordinate, and dependent powers"—a crucial concept since he repeats the phrase within the same short paragraph—constitute "intermediary canals through which power flows." The nobility is a conduit that channels the sovereign's power and thereby limits it. For Montesquieu, the existence of a nobility that surrounds the king and tempers his power is what distinguishes monarchy from despotism. The latter is the rule of a single individual without any constraints or limitations, that is, without an aristocracy that diminishes the prince's absolute power by serving as a counterweight and by incarnating the nation's fundamental laws. Here Montesquieu adumbrates the admiration he will express for the constitutional monarchy in England and for the Frankish model of the king as "first among equals." Although Montesquieu clearly labels despotism as an Eastern phenomenon (we remember the harem in *The Persian Letters*), he also suggests that a European monarch who destroys his aristocracy would become a tyrant, too. His lurking fear of despotism explains Montesquieu's consistently negative judgments on Louis XIV who had increased the powers of the crown by reducing those of the nobility.

To each of these three governments (four if we distinguish the two types of republics) corresponds one particular form of civic behavior that reinforces the nature of that one government but not of the others. Montesquieu locates the appropriate principle in the "human passions" (3:1:251) that motivate the citizens living under each particular government. In a democratic republic the activating principle is civic virtue. Without it, the two forces most inimical to the equality that defines a democracy, ambition and avarice, would rule. In an aristocratic republic, moderation is the motivation since it prevents the upper class from oppressing the lower classes. The ruling passion in a monarchy is honor, defined as "the ingrained attitude of every individual and of every class" (3:6:256). Honor permits a nobleman or group of nobles to stand up to the king and thereby limit his absolute power. The ambition that is dangerous in republics is beneficial in the monarchy. Evoking a mechanical metaphor, Montesquieu illustrates how honor functions like gravity: "it is like the operation of the universe where one force [centrifugal] pushes everything away from the center and a gravitational force [centripetal] pulls them back. Honor moves all the parts of the body politic. It connects them by its very activity, and it happens that everyone contributes to the common good while thinking he is going about his private business" (3:7:257). Fear is the operative principle in a despotic state. Everyone fears the ruler who knows no limitation on his absolute power.

These principles or laws form the basis of Montesquieu's radically new (for the eighteenth century) way of understanding how governments are constituted. Each is defined by the nature of its ruling process, which in turn depends on a mind-set that is shared by its citizens. Other historians of this epoch described governments and nations by reference to their external appearances, by the men and events that marked their history. Montesquieu is analytic rather than descriptive.

He is trying to uncover the deep causes that explain the surface phenomena.

But where do these different mind-sets or principles come from? And how do they come about? Dealing with education and the formation of customs, book 4 examines how citizens learn to behave in a manner appropriate to the government under which they live. Noblemen living in a monarchy learn "that it is necessary to have a certain nobility in one's virtues, a certain frankness in one's mores, and a certain politeness in one's manners" (4:2:262). Even though "there is nothing that honor prescribes more to noblemen than serving their prince in war" (4:2:264), that same honor cannot be abused by the ruler. Therefore it constrains him because "this honor tells us that the prince should never order us to commit an action that dishonors us because that very action would make us incapable of serving him" (4:2:264). Under a despot, education would be forbidden since "knowledge is dangerous there" (4:3:265). Tyrants detest educated citizens; they much prefer fearful slaves. In contrast, education is essential in republics because their citizens have the difficult duty of renouncing self-interest and promoting love of country and its laws (4:5:267). Montesquieu generally bemoans the loss of this civic ideal in modern times, although he does cite one rare leader who was able to realize the social education of his people: "One legislator and honest man has formed a people in whom honesty seems as natural as bravery among the Spartans. William Penn is a veritable Lycurgus" (4:6:268). The Quakers of Pennsylvania had already in the eighteenth century acquired their reputation for bringing the highest moral principles to their civic duties.

Book 7 examines the difficulty of maintaining these principles. Here, as in his *Considerations,* Montesquieu is acutely aware that states, like people, are living organisms that go through a cycle of vigorous growth followed by inevitable decline. He focuses on the related topics of luxury and women to illustrate this dilemma.

Democracies should have little if any luxury since it is contrary to their principle of equality. The work ethic and the desire to live by the sweat of one's own brow displace the need for luxury. "In those republics where equality is not entirely lost, the spirit of commerce, work, and virtue combine so that everyone can and wants to live by his own accomplishments. Consequently there is little luxury" (7:2:334). The danger for a republic is that luxury encourages the self-serving and selfish behaviors that can destroy the state: "To the extent that luxury penetrates a republic, its spirit turns toward selfishness" (7:2:335). An aristocratic republic finds luxury a problem because "there the aristocrats are rich and nonetheless they should not spend conspicuously" (7:3:335). Conspicuous consumption is contrary to the spirit of moderation proper to that form of republic. Luxury is, however, "singularly appropriate for monarchies" (7:4:336). Indeed, an economy that is typically monarchical thrives on producing deluxe items for a privileged few. According to Montesquieu, "for a monarchy to endure, luxury has to increase, from the worker to the artisan, [through] the businessman, [to] the nobles, the judges, the lords, the richest financial speculators, the princes. Without that, all is lost" (7:4:336). Using China as his illustration, Montesquieu argues that luxury in a despotism is pernicious because "the spirit of work and economy is as important there as it is in any republic" (7:6:339). A victim like every other nation of the cycle of rise and fall, China at first displayed "virtue, attention, vigilance" (7:7:340). But later these characteristics were replaced by "corruption, luxury, laziness, soft living." As these examples show, luxury in itself has no fixed value or significance in Montesquieu's scheme. Reacting to each situation differently, the same luxury produces diverse results given different governments and principles: "Republics end in luxury, monarchies in poverty" (7:4:337).

Having considered luxury as an economic issue, Montesquieu slips into a discussion of its moral connotations. In English the sense of luxury as "lasciviousness" is archaic, but in French this sense still remains strong. This semantic link between money and morality allows Montesquieu to consider the economic impact that women exert on society. Not only were women prime clients for luxury products but they also were sexual temptations in the gallant French society that Montesquieu knew so well and that provided the ideological backdrop for the *Laws*. Again, social context determines the meaning or significance that luxury will take. "In despotic states, women do not introduce luxury but are themselves an object of luxury. They have to be very much slaves" (7:9:341). On the other hand, in republics, "women are free according to the laws and captive according to the mores. Luxury is banished and with it corruption and vice" (7:9:341). Here Montesquieu begins a long disquisition on sexual misbehavior by women in classical Rome that demonstrates the extent to which laws and mores are interdependent. Laws against adultery like the *lex Julia* do not indicate respect for morality; rather, they indicate how depraved the Romans really were to need such laws (7:13:345). Montesquieu's reading of classical Rome is more subtle than simple. No phenomenon has a single, exclusive meaning. Each requires examination in its own particular context. Inextricably intertwined, laws and mores exert a strong reciprocal influence upon each other. "The [Roman] court of law maintained mores under the republic. But those same mores maintained the court" (7:10:342). Laws may be enacted even though there is no real public consensus to do what those laws require. Lacking public support, such laws are disobeyed. This gap between the ideal of the law and the reality of public behavior pushes the state a bit further along its downward spiral of decline.

The final book of part 1 deals with corruption of the principles of government since that is how a state's decline really begins. In a democracy, corruption starts when "people lose the spirit of equality but also when they take on the spirit of extreme equality" (8:2:349). The arbitrary use of power, signaling the loss of civic moderation, is the onset of corruption for aristocratic republics (8:5). A despotic state cannot decline. It is always corrupt "by nature" because its principle, fear, is vicious and based on "internal vice" (8:10). This condemnation of despotism runs throughout the entire treatise and marks one of the rare value judgments that Montesquieu makes about the social and political phenomena he is analyzing. In a monarchy, the loss of aristocratic prerogatives and privileges marks the beginning of the end (8:6:354–55). Here a delicate balance hinges on the nobility's sense of honor as the power broker between the monarch and his subjects, limiting the former while representing the latter. One phrase sums up Montesquieu's recognition of how Louis XIV upset that equilibrium: "A monarchy is lost when the prince, assimilating everything to himself, calls the state to his capital, the capital to his court, the court to his individual person" (8:6:355). For Montesquieu, the decline of the French monarchy began paradoxically with its strongest king who wielded the most power for the longest period of time.

To avoid decline as long as possible, states should not exceed their optimal size. Republics should remain small (8:16). When they get too large, they lose their spirit of moderation and self-interest runs rampant. A monarchy can be middle-sized since distance functions like an intermediary power and diminishes the sovereign's absolute power (8:17). Any large, far-flung empire would have to be despotic since there is no other way to rule such an expanse effectively (8:19). Montesquieu's law of size ordains "that the state will change its spirit to the degree that its borders contract or expand" (8:20:365). After this mechanical formula, a more fluid metaphor expresses Montesquieu's fear that the French monarchy's policy of expansion was moving the nation toward tyranny: "Rivers throw themselves into the sea. Monarchies lose themselves in despotism" (8:17:364). That imagery captures the irresistible force of the elements evoked. Change is natural and inevitable; its onset as well as its stages are as predictable and as inevitable as the flow of water from a mountain top to the ocean.

Now let us return to books 5 and 6 which I skipped to avoid interrupting the discussion of forming, maintaining, and losing principles. Montesquieu often uses the chiasmus as a structural or rhetorical device. This pattern of *a:b::b':a'* is one of the articulations that my outline helps bring to light. Not only does Montesquieu avoid monotony by shifting to another subject, he also creates a feeling of satisfaction in his readers when he returns to a topic already discussed and whose conclusion he has temporarily postponed.

The responsibility for inspiring and inculcating the appropriate spirit for each type of government falls to the legislator, whether that be an individual such as Lycurgus, a group such as the Roman Senate, or even something as vague as a national consensus. The source of republican virtue is the love of equality and, more importantly, of frugality which "limits the desire for acquisitions to what necessity requires for one's family and the superfluous asks for one's country" (5:3:275). A mercantile republic can be rich and thrive, however, because almost paradoxically commerce can preserve the spirit of frugality in the midst of wealth: "the spirit of commerce brings with it the spirit of frugality, economy, moderation, hard work, wisdom, tranquility, orderliness, and discipline. Consequently, while this spirit endures, the wealth it produces has no ill effect. It becomes harmful when the excess of wealth destroys this spirit of commerce" (5:6:280). Such a litany of virtues reveals why so many eighteenth-century *philosophes* extolled commerce. They saw international trade as a force that promoted peace and reduced the risk of war. In their eyes, economic ties would create an international business community based on mutual trust and cooperation, thus freeing men of the dangerously narrow nationalistic interests that inspire conflict.

A final method of inculcating republican principles is the return to the past. The legislator should know that "to remind men of ancient maxims is usually to bring them back to virtue" (5:7:281). Like his near contemporary in England, Edmund Burke, Montesquieu is a true conservative in that he does not favor change per se: "Usually therefore old institutions are correctives, and new ones abuses" (5:7:281–82).

All republics are based on equality. While democratic equality is informed by frugality, the aristocratic republic should base its equality on moderation. This is difficult to achieve since an oligarchy, unlike a democracy, is by definition built on the "extreme inequality between those who govern and those who are governed" (5:8:284). The same solution works for both, however. Being the "profession of equals" (5:8:286), trade is appropriate in all republics because one of its effects is to produce or increase equality. Monarchy, in contrast, requires a hereditary nobility that would give stability to its principle, honor, and allow the nobles to be the link between "the power of the prince and the weakness of the people" (5:9:288). There are two striking passages that deal with despotism. The first is an entire chapter that consists of two short sentences: "When the savages of Louisiana want some fruit, they cut the tree down at its base and gather the fruit. That is despotic government" (5:13:292). For Montesquieu, the stupidity of this behavior requires no commentary, its obvious shortsightedness no additional condemnation. The second passage evokes those Eastern harems where all depends on whim and passing fancy: "The ruling family resembles the state. It is too weak and its head too strong; it seems immense and is reduced to nothing. . . . It is easier to imagine that some Eastern harem intrigue is at work here, where artifice, meanness, and guile rule in silence and hide in deep night, where an old prince, becoming every day more and more senile, is the prime prisoner of his own palace" (5:14:297). The encomium of commerce contrasts with the critique of tyranny. Republics encourage their citizens to develop the business virtues that support the state while the despotic nation, ruled by a man jealous of any challenge to his total authority, prefers a lethargy that will prove fatal.

Like the legislator, the magistrate has a decisive influence on public mores. Judges should mete out punishments that accord with and sustain the spirit most fitting to each polity. Since it is based on an immense interweaving of rank and privilege, monarchy requires a vast judicial system to administer the "great interests" put in play by honor (6:1). Republican judges should be constant and invariable while despotic ones are petty tyrants to all beneath them: "In despotic states, there is no law: the judge is his own law. In monarchies, there is a law. When it is clear, the judge follows it; when it is not, he seeks out its spirit. In a republic it is in the nature of the constitution that the judges follow the letter of the law" (6:3:311). Only under the monarchy does

Montesquieu allow magistrates to perform the intricate task of interpretation and of setting precedent that we recognize today as normal.

Montesquieu goes on to discuss the nature of punishment. These chapters belong to an important phase of Enlightenment thought, the movement to reform penal codes and to establish the principle that punishments, while remaining sufficiently harsh to deter crime, ought nonetheless to be humane. One example will suffice to illustrate what criminal justice was like in the eighteenth century. In 1757, two years after Montesquieu's death, a horrible public spectacle took place in Paris: the execution of the man who had attempted to assassinate Louis XV. Tried and found guilty, Damiens was condemned to death. Before that, however, his arms and legs were pulled out of their sockets and his bones broken (all while he was still alive). His internal organs were then cut out, heaped on his chest, and set aflame. The ordeal lasted over an hour and attracted a huge throng that found the proceedings a kind of entertainment.[4] Indeed, executions in the eighteenth century were considered public spectacles intended both to amuse and to instruct the observers. Although this punishment was extreme in degree, it was not unusual or different in nature from what was meted out to ordinary criminals. With Damiens's torture in mind, we can better appreciate Montesquieu's discussion of the judicial "question," that is, the legal use of torture to interrogate suspects before they were put on trial and to obtain evidence that could be introduced in court.

Chapter 17 is a short, two-paragraph rebuttal of torture as an acceptable judicial procedure. It is worth analyzing briefly because it is problematic. Montesquieu does not have recourse to his usual erudition, nor does he make an intellectual condemnation of torture. Rather, he employs irony and thereby risks misinterpretation. The confusion his method often incites reminds us that Montesquieu can be elusive and enigmatic. Although men are often mean, he begins, the law assumes they are good. Thus, two witnesses suffice in court whether they are trustworthy or not. He implies, but does not state, that torture is equally unreliable. Recognizing that so many fine writers have opposed torture, he does not presume to add to what they have argued. At best, he concedes, torture "could be appropriate to" a despotic government which is always corrupt anyway. And then he notes that ancient Greece and Rome tortured slaves. . . . But rational discussion of such an issue is impossible. Any effort to understand it should simply cease: "But I hear the voice of nature which cries out against me" (6:17:329). Heeding that call, Montesquieu abruptly terminates his chapter and thereby relegates torture to a realm beyond any attempt at explanation where, he apparently hopes, it will disappear forever.

Second Part: Books 9–13

The second part of the *Laws* opens with two books on war. For Montesquieu, true power is less the ability to conquer others than to defend oneself (9:6:374). He notes that being subject to international law, at least in theory, modern conquests are less destructive than they were in ancient times. "I leave it to others to judge how much better we have become. Here we must thank our modern times, current reason, today's religion, our philosophy, our mores" (10:3:379). Montesquieu does not reject the right of war and conquest, but he does impose obligations on it. For example, "A conqueror should repair a part of the evils he has done. I define thus the right of conquest: a necessary, legitimate, but unfortunate right that always leaves an enormous debt to be paid in order to be reconciled with human nature" (10:4:381). A hard-nosed realist, Montesquieu deals with the disagreeable facts of human history as well as the "ought to's." Here I must again note his recurrent fear that monarchy will slip too easily into despotism because of its bellicose policies. He writes: "Such is the necessary condition of a conquering monarchy: luxury in the capital, misery in the outlying provinces, and abundance on the most distant frontiers. It is like our planet: fire is in the center, greenery on the surface, and cold, sterile, arid land in between" (10:9:385).

The following three books deal with liberty which Montesquieu defines as "the right to do all that laws permit" (11:3:395). Liberty consists in being able "to do what one should want to do, and not being forced to do what one should not want to do." Only in moderate governments does Montesquieu recognize political liberty, for only there does he find the necessary equilibrium of powers that assures freedom under the laws. As he puts it, "In order that no one abuse power, it is necessary that, by the arrangement of things, power block power" (11:4:395). This theory of equilibrium leads to the famous chapter (11:6) on the British constitution which so influenced our Founding Fathers.[5] Montesquieu's somewhat erroneous explanation of the separation of powers in the English parliamentary system eventually led to the checks-and-balances of the American Constitution.[6]

There are three types of power: "making laws, executing public decisions, and judging crimes or disputes among individuals" (11:6:397), which is to say legislative, executive, and judicial power, respectively. Although "every man who has a free soul should govern himself" (11:6:399), that is impractical. Hence the need for representatives in a republican legislature, whether it be elective (democratic) or hereditary (aristocratic). Montesquieu has the typical eighteenth-century wariness about the common people's ability to handle public affairs.

For Montesquieu, the executive is inherently weaker than the legislature: "since execution has limitations by its very nature, it is unnecessary to limit it" (11:6:403). While the executive's person is sacred and inviolable, his advisers are not. "But since he who executes cannot do so poorly without bad advisers . . . these can be pursued and punished" (11:6:403). On this point Montesquieu is very much the product of his monarchical environment that always considered the king himself sacred. If wrong is done in the king's name, it must be his ministers who are guilty. The possibility of impeachment, added to the American Constitution, would seem too democratic for Montesquieu. Putting the king on trial, as was done during the French Revolution, would have been inconceivable to him.

These three powers are so intertwined that each single one can function only in conjunction with the other two: "These three powers should constitute a rest or an inaction. However, when by the necessary movement of things they are obliged to move, they will be forced to do so together" (11:6:405). This harmonious cooperation is obviously a minimalist government, the counterbalance of whose forces provides a guarantee of liberty and a bulwark against tyranny.

Such an equilibrium is a republican ideal. With all power concentrated in one individual, despotism permits no such balance and therefore provides no liberty for its subjects. Similarly, a monarchy tends to concentrate power in the prince, thus risking its equilibrium. In addition, based on its ruling passion of honor, monarchy has pursuit of glory, not liberty, as its first object. This glory can, however, lead to a "spirit of liberty" (11:7:408) which, while not liberty itself, will produce "equally great things" and just as much happiness for its citizens. The problem of whether liberty can exist under a monarch prompts Montesquieu to consider the Germanic nations, a topic he will return to at great length in the sixth and last part of the *Laws*. Here he briefly sketches their progress toward liberty. After conquering Rome (the section's themes of liberty and warfare here join), the German tribes evolved from a direct democracy in which "the entire nation could assemble" (11:8:409) to government by representatives. Slowly intermediary powers grew up, checking each other and working in concert: "The custom was established to accord letters of manumission [freedom]. Soon the civil liberty of the people, the prerogatives of the nobility and clergy, and the power of the kings found themselves in such harmony that I do not think there has been in any part of Europe a government on earth so well tempered as this one during the time that it existed" (11:8:409). Out of that original conquest came a monarchy that was able to secure liberty for its subjects. Montesquieu approvingly notes, "It is admirable that the corruption of the government of a conquering people formed the best kind of government that men have been able to imagine" (11:8:409).

After the examples of the English constitution and the Germanic origins of the French monarchy comes the subject that Montesquieu could never resist: Rome. Because that is so vast a topic, I can mention no more than three of Montesquieu's examples of the struggle between power and liberty. In his typically elliptical manner Montesquieu alludes to the overthrow of the tyrant Tarquin in early Rome. By acquiring too much power, Tarquin abused his authority and therefore provoked his own fall: "His power increased . . . he usurped the power of the people; he made laws without the people, even against them. He would have gathered the three powers in himself, but the people remembered for a moment that they were the legislator, and Tarquin was no more" (11:12:413). This retelling is too rapid and literary: "Tarquin was no more" is an example of litotes, a rhetorical figure much used by French classical writers. It deliberately understates its point in order to produce a more powerful effect. The phrase means that Tarquin was removed from power and executed, but it does not indicate how that happened. That voluntary silence or understatement suggests how inevitable and unstoppable Tarquin's demise was. Anachronistically, Montesquieu imposes on this ancient power struggle his own concept of constitutional balances that its protagonists would not have recognized. Still, the case does illustrate the danger of not separating powers and how the mechanism of counterbalance reestablishes political stability. The second example involves the decemvirs under the Republic. "Ten men in the republic possessed by themselves all the legislative power, all the executive power, all the judicial power. Rome saw itself subjected to a tyranny as cruel as Tarquin's" (11:15:417–18). Only a spectacular and moving incident could redress this imbalance. That impetus was provided by Virginia, whose father chose to kill her rather than allow her to be raped by one of the decemvirs. Sex and politics mix in a most explosive combination. Although Montesquieu does not emphasize the former element, it provides the spark for political action: "The spectacle of Virginia's death, immolated by her father to purity and liberty, made the decimvirs' power vanish. Every man found himself free because every man was offended. Everyone became a citizen because everyone became a father. The Senate and the people regained a liberty that had been confided to those ridiculous tyrants" (11:15:418). Third, in discussing the abuse of judiciary power, Montesquieu sees "liberty . . . in the center and tyranny at the extremities" of the Roman empire. Taking advantage of the distance that separated them from Rome, provincial judges combined all three powers in themselves and became "the pashas of the Republic" (11:19:428). Eastern despotism again furnishes the reference point for the dangers that menace liberty.

Book 12 treats liberty in its relation to the private citizen. The "triumph of liberty" (12:4:433) consists of punishments that are not arbitrary but rather suited to the crime. Rule by law is so fundamental to liberty that even a man in prison can be considered free if the laws have been correctly applied in his case: "in a state that had the best possible laws, a man who had been tried and who was to be hanged the next day would be freer than a pasha in Turkey" (12:3:432). Montesquieu refuses to condone civil punishments for infractions of religious laws (12:4). He defends freedom of thought, even if those thoughts are criminal (12:11). Freedom of speech should be protected unless it leads directly to crime: "Thus a man who goes into a public place to exhort the citizens to revolt becomes guilty of treason because his words are joined to and participate in actions. It is not the words that are punished but the acts in which words were used. Words only become crimes when they prepare, accompany, or follow a criminal action" (12:12:443). This was quite a liberal position to adopt in an age of *lettres de cachet* (arbitrary orders to imprison someone), institutionalized spying on the mails, and strict censorship of all written materials. By expressing thoughts that would qualify as modern and liberal, Montesquieu reveals his personal courage. Here his scholarship is not disembodied and dry as dust; here his voice is committed, *engagé* in the ongoing political struggle of the eighteenth century.

Book 13 considers taxes and other fiscal matters as a function of liberty. Like everything else, money belongs to a web of moral attitudes. Here Montesquieu exhibits a social conscience and sense of responsibility that may surprise even socialist thinkers. Referring to a poll tax in classical Athens, he says: "The tax was just . . . if it was not proportional to wealth, it was proportional to needs. They decided that everyone deserved a bare minimum that should not be taxed. What was useful came next and should be taxed, but less than the superfluous. And the amount of the tax on the superfluous prevented it [i.e., a confiscatory tax on superfluous wealth]" (13:7:462).

It is well known that eighteenth-century *philosophes* such as Voltaire and Diderot extolled the virtues of merchants and sang the praises of commerce. Book 13 gives us other examples of the privileged status of commerce in Enlightenment thought. Montesquieu traces the positive impact of businessmen through the taxes they paid to the state. He argues that they contribute both financially and politically to the creation of moderate governments: "The natural pay of a moderate government is the tax on goods. . . . Thus we should regard the businessman both as a salesman of the state and a creditor of all its citizens" (13:14:468). He recognizes that indirect taxes, hidden in the selling price of an item, are invisible and therefore most easily accepted by the public. The modern French tax code follows this advice closely in imposing a value-added tax on most items.

On the other hand, Montesquieu denounces in no uncertain terms the contemporary tax collectors who were able to enrich themselves while impoverishing the state both fiscally and morally: "All is lost when the lucrative profession of tax collector succeeds in becoming an honored profession because of money" (13:20:473). A nation's moral fiber is destroyed when money reverses its traditional priorities, undermines its values, and sets up false standards for judging honor and success. "That is not good in a republic," Montesquieu writes and adds that it is just as bad in a monarchy: "Disgust seizes all the other classes. Honor loses all consideration, the slow and natural ways of distinguishing oneself are no longer effective, and the government is wounded in its principle" (13:20:473). Under the eighteenth-century French system, tax collectors were called "farmers." They were something like franchise holders who purchased the right to collect taxes. They guaranteed a fixed amount of revenue to the state and kept the difference between that fixed sum and whatever amount they could extract from the people. They became enormously wealthy even though the state's finances never improved and the people suffered from wholesale extortion and poverty. Montesquieu argues that money, especially in such large amounts held by a few, disrupts the normal balance of powers in any state and thus leads to despotism: "Since he who has money is always the master of the other, the tax collector becomes despotic even with the prince. He is not the legislator, but he can force the legislator to enact laws" (13:19:472). Although at first glance the connection is not obvious, Montesquieu does succeed in melding his taxonomy of governments and his concern with the moral underpinning of a nation into his discussion of liberty and taxes. This is not the only time taxes and liberty are such close neighbors in eighteenth-century political discourse. Taxation and representation would soon become a rallying cry of the American Revolution.

Third Part: Books 14–19

The third part of the *Laws* contains another one of the theories for which Montesquieu is most famous, his theory of how climate influences human behavior. Let the reader beware, however. While Montesquieu seems at times to overstate the case for physical causation, he is fully cognizant in other places of the limitations of this theory.

In the first of the four books devoted to climate, Montesquieu advances the idea that purely physical factors like heat and cold exert a decisive influence on human actions. He begins with an empirical statement based on physics: "Cold air shortens the extremities of the external fibers of our body; this increases their tension. . . . Warm air, on the contrary, loosens the fibers' extremities and lengthens them. Therefore it diminishes their strength and their tension" (14:2:474). These physical principles established, Montesquieu extends them into the moral sphere. Cold climates produce a more vigorous race since cold causes the blood to circulate faster and the heart to pump harder, producing more self-confidence and courage. His chain of physical causes and moral consequences culminates thus: "People in warm climates are as timid as old men while those in cold countries are as brave as young ones" (14:2:475). A simple biology experiment was at the origin of these physico-moral speculations. Like Voltaire, who installed an experimental laboratory in his house at Cirey, Benjamin Franklin, whose scientific experiments are well known, and so many other eighteenth-century *philosophes*, Montesquieu was an amateur scientist who brought his technical curiosity to all his other interests. Here he describes his use of scientific method: "I observed the surface of a sheep's tongue, especially the spot where, to the naked eye, it appears to be covered with little tips. With a microscope I saw little hairs on these tips. . . . I froze half the tongue and observed, with the naked eye, that the tips had diminished considerably. . . . As the tongue thawed, the tips could be seen to stand up" (14:2:476).

With the help of the experimental sciences that were then coming into their own as independent disciplines and valid sources of knowledge, Montesquieu was seeking a rational basis for his historical and cultural study. He wanted to discover *laws* like those of physics that would explain different human behaviors. He notes, for example, "I have seen opera in England and Italy. It is the same opera with the same actors. But the same music produces such different effects on those two nations, one being so calm, the other so passionate, that it seems inconceivable" (14:2:476). Today we might object that these observations are well-worn stereotypes about national character or even culture. More than 200 years ago they were a good deal fresher and more convincing. Furthermore, Montesquieu is discussing evidence he has found as he seeks a scientific basis for measuring human differences. He talks about "degrees of sensibility" and wants to know if they correspond to the geographer's "degrees of latitude." From music he jumps to the pleasures of love, still measuring moral differences with a geographer's compass and a libertine's wit: "In southern climes, a delicate, weak, but sensitive machine [the body] is given up to amorous activity which, in a harem, constantly swells and ebbs. . . . In the northern countries, a healthy, well constructed but heavy machine finds its pleasures in anything that can put its spirits into motion. . . . In temperate climates, you will see nations inconstant in their mores, in their vices, and in their virtues. The climate there does not have a stable enough character to fix the people" (14:2:477). This north-south dichotomy in both the physical and the political domains became a commonplace after Montesquieu in writers such as Mme de Staël, Chateaubriand, and the later romantics. For Montesquieu, physical determination matches a favorite belief in Germanic liberties: "In the time of the Romans, the people of northern Europe lived without art, without education, almost without laws. Nonetheless, thanks to nothing more than the good sense attached to the clumsy fibers of those climates, they resisted Roman power with admirable wisdom until that moment when they left their forests to destroy it" (14:3:478).

Today many readers notice only the overstatements in Montesquieu's theory of climate. Surely he did go too far in seeing a simplistic, one-to-one correlation between climate and human behavior. I would note in his defense, however, that he was, if not the originator of this theory, at least one of the first and surely the most important writer to give it wide circulation and credence in the eighteenth century. The subsequent growth of scientific knowledge has imposed a number of important qualifications on this idea. Nonetheless, it is only fair to acknowledge that Montesquieu himself expressed this theory with a good deal more subtlety in a number of other passages. He makes a key correction when he claims not straightforward causation but rather that differing physical environments favor distinct behaviors: "It was the different needs in the different climates that formed the different ways of living. These different ways of living in turn formed diverse types of laws" (14:8:483–84).

This sentence concludes a chapter on sobriety and on why nations drink either wine or water. Muhammad's interdiction against wine is, for Montesquieu, a law of the Arabian climate. By replacing religious motivation with a natural explanation, Montesquieu is treading along a dangerous path. His scientific objectivity has far-reaching implications for religious thought. Are the Hebrew dietary laws as dictated by Moses simply natural to a certain climate rather than inspired by God? What about Catholicism's commandments about fasting and abstinence? Montesquieu does not voice these questions but they are nonetheless insidiously present in the fabric of his inquiry.

Similarly, he considers suicide not as a sin but as a climatic phenomenon. Throughout the eighteenth century Englishmen were considered morbidly melancholy and prone to suicide, a disposition we today might offhandedly attribute to dreary weather and rainy winters without sunshine. Montesquieu has a different theory: "This action [suicide] was the effect of education among the Romans. It was connected to their way of thinking and their customs. Among the English, it is the effect of a sickness. It is connected to the physical state of their machine [body] and is independent of any other cause" (14:12:486). When examined more closely and carefully, what Montesquieu is saying about how climate has affected history can make a good deal of sense.

Book 15 examines the connections between climate and slavery. Montesquieu sees the East in general as having a tropical climate and a penchant for despotism, while temperate Europe is the home of liberty and moderate governments. In a celebrated and often cited chapter, Montesquieu protests against the black slave trade. Ironically, he deforms the arguments in favor of slavery. He notes, for example, that "Sugar would be too expensive if the plant that produced it were not

cultivated by slaves" (15:5:494). Tongue-in-cheek in Voltairian fashion, he offers pitiful justifications that in fact undermine slavery rather
than defend it, as with the remark that "small minds exaggerate the
injustice done to Africans." Simultaneously sarcastic and ludic, this
chapter is liable to misinterpretation precisely because its denunciation
is mocking and indirect. Taken in the context of the surrounding chapters, however, the intention is perfectly clear. Unfortunately, some
readers have mistaken these woefully inadequate reasons for legitimate
ones and thus completely missed the point of Montesquieu's mock "defense" which conceals, in fact, an indirect but powerful attack.

For Montesquieu, slavery is natural in despotic states and is a major
danger elsewhere because it debases men and literally transforms them
into beasts: "Nothing brings us closer to the condition of animals than
to always see free men and not to be one. Such people are the natural
enemies of society. Having too many of them would be dangerous"
(15:13:500). Humane treatment can mitigate the worst effects of slavery, however, and thus avoid its most dangerous pitfalls. Montesquieu
notes that only when the Romans lost all human sentiment for their
slaves did civil war break out (15:16:502). Thus, Roman slavery illustrates the intricate relationship of customs and laws that will be
discussed again in book 19. When Rome was regulated by humane
customs slavery was not too oppressive: "Mores were enough to maintain the slaves' fidelity; laws were not needed" (15:16:502). When
Rome grew into an empire riddled with luxury and pride, it lost its
compassion and had to enact laws that were "terrible" in both senses:
"since there were no more mores, they needed laws. It required terrible
ones to ensure the safety of those cruel masters who lived among their
slaves as if among their enemies" (15:16:502). Slavery puts any government to the test. As Montesquieu astutely observes, slavery corrupts
the master "because he contracts with his slaves all sorts of bad habits;
inadvertently he grows accustomed to not exercising any moral virtues;
he becomes haughty, quick-tempered, hard, angry, voluptuous, cruel"
(15:1:490). Seen as a form of despotism, slavery is inimical to nations
that would be free. Even severe laws cannot save the nation or the
people whose spirit and mores have been corrupted by it.

Book 16 continues the analysis of slavery while significantly shifting
its focal point. It transforms the subject to domestic servitude and from
this perspective discusses women who might be considered the equivalent of slaves in the eighteenth century. This book deserves close attention since critics are divided on whether Montesquieu is a misogynist

or an early feminist.[7] Whatever conclusion one reaches, it cannot be denied that Montesquieu is quite ahead of his time in initiating a debate on the status of women. Speaking about polygamy, he makes a crucial statement that can be applied to many other passages throughout the *Laws*: "In all this, I am not justifying these customs, I am only offering the reasons behind them" (16:4:511). Except on rare and therefore noteworthy occasions, Montesquieu refuses to make value judgments about the phenomena he is investigating. He remains the detached, rational analyst rather than the emotional polemicist. Therefore, readers have to be careful not to confuse his scholarly desire to be impartial with his personal feelings.

Chapter 9 makes an explicit connection between despotism and the situation of women: "women's servitude conforms quite well to the genius of despotic government which loves to abuse everything" (16:9:514). Female intrigues are so complex that they would be fatal to a husband or a state (16:9:515). We remember not only the episode of Virginia and the decemvirs but more importantly *The Persian Letters* where the seraglio seethed with conspiracies. Montesquieu proposes a hypothetical situation that mingles politics and female sexuality: "Let us suppose for a moment that the frothy spirit and the indiscretions, the likes and dislikes of our women, their passions great and small were transported to an Eastern government, including all the activity and the liberty that women know among us. Who is the father who could be tranquil for one moment about his daughter? Everywhere suspicious men, everywhere enemies. The state would be rocked, you would see blood flow freely" (16:9:515). Here the gallant tone and the bantering reference to female indiscretions are not far from the tragic resonances of the novel. The conjunction between fact and fiction is provocative. Is Roxane able to rebel against Usbek only because and to the extent that she possesses a European and not an Oriental character? Montesquieu's harem still hides some secrets just as his attitude toward women remains complex.

An extremely short book 17 picks up the theoretical issues of book 14 and completes the chiasmus structure that was mentioned earlier. Here the focus is on liberty. According to Montesquieu, northern climates are vigorous and libertarian while southern climes tend toward slavery: " there was in cold climates a certain strength of mind and body which made men capable of actions that were long, difficult, great, and audacious. . . . We should not be surprised, then, that the cowardice of people from warm climates has almost always made them slaves and the courage of those from cold climates has kept them free" (17:2:523). Since Montesquieu maintains that Asia has no temperate zone while Europe does, he can relate climate to liberty: "That is the prime reason for the weakness of Asia and the strength of Europe, the liberty of Europe and the servitude of Asia, a cause that to my knowledge has never before been noticed" (17:3:526). The distinction remains valid even in the ways these two continents and two climates conquer: "The peoples of northern Europe conquered it as free men. The peoples of northern Asia conquered it as slaves and only triumphed for a master" (17:5:527). Montesquieu's enthusiasm for northern liberty is almost limitless. He calls Scandinavia the "source of liberty in Europe" (17:5:528). The North is "the producer of tools that break chains forged in the south. There are formed those valiant nations that leave their country to destroy tyrants and slaves" (17:5:528).

After climate Montesquieu turns to geography. Fertile countries usually have a single ruler while sterile ones tend toward government by many (18:1). Prosperity is less a question of natural resources than of politics: "Countries are not cultivated because of their fertility but because of their liberty" (18:3:532). Mountain states are the abode of liberty since they can be defended easily and attacked only with difficulty (18:2). Matters of fertility and production lead Montesquieu to anticipate a subject, money, that he will develop at greater length later in part 4: "Working the land demands the use of currency. Agriculture presumes many arts and much knowledge. We always see the arts, knowledge, and [physical] needs walking in step" (18:15:539). While civilization may grow thanks to money, liberty does not: "Among peoples who do not have a currency, everyone has few needs and satisfies them easily and equally. Thus their equality is obligatory, and their leaders are not despotic" (18:17:540). The frugality of the Troglodytes was the source of their liberty. Montesquieu does not resolve the obvious contradictions between civilization, as measured in terms of money, and liberty. His comments suggest that a modern society cannot really be free since it cannot do without money. Rather than attempt some middle road or synthesis, Montesquieu multiplies his observations, concentrating on the details and putting aside the difficulty of reconciling them all in the end. While making the *Laws* rich and diverse, such myopic concentration on the particulars at the expense of the whole creates confusion. Questions left unanswered provoke a stimulating reaction but they also preclude any conclusion about the author's final opinion. They oblige us to read Montesquieu as a single text, seeing each chapter, like each separate work, only as another approximation of his ultimate idea.

In book 19 he passes from physical factors (climate, geography) to moral causes. While customs and mores are intangible, they are nonetheless critical elements in the formation of a nation. Culture is as solid and as real as any physical factor. This solidity is demonstrated by Montesquieu's choice of an atmospheric metaphor to illustrate a moral situation: "Liberty was itself unbearable to those peoples who were not accustomed to it. Thus clean air is sometimes harmful to those who have lived in swampy areas" (19:2:557). Custom is the second law of a nation, but it often takes priority over the first because it operates at a deeper, more instinctive, and more powerful level: "It is for the legislator to follow the spirit of a nation when it is not contrary to the principles of the government. For we never do anything better than when we do it freely and in accord with our natural tendencies" (19:5:559). Consequently, when "those who govern establish things that shock the nation's way of thinking," their actions can be considered a "tyranny" (19:3:557) even though they are acting legally. For Montesquieu, mores are the most powerful of laws.

Chapter 4 contains an important reformulation and definition of what is meant by the term "general spirit." That spirit, like the spirit of the laws, is the totality of influences that form a nation:

Several things govern men: climate, religion, laws, the government's slogans, examples from the past, mores, and habits. From all that a general spirit is formed as a result.

To the degree that, in every nation, one of these causes acts with more force, the others are diminished by just as much. (19.4.558)

Often forgotten, perhaps because it was placed in a separate paragraph, that last sentence is critical. For Montesquieu, all causative factors are interconnected. Increase one and the others diminish proportionately. Montesquieu's recognition of multiple and interdependent causes here provides an important corrective to the apparent rigidity of the theory of climate as expressed elsewhere. Climate is only one in that series of factors that together determine the general spirit of a nation.

Women play a large role in establishing a nation's customs, even if it is not always a flattering one. According to Montesquieu, "The society of women spoils mores and forms taste" (19:8:560). Women create fashions that, although frivolous, support commercial activity.

Montesquieu distinguishes the good effects of vanity from the pernicious effects of pride. On one hand, there are "those good things without number that result from vanity: luxury, industry, arts, fashion, politeness, taste. On the other hand are the numerous evils born of the pride of certain nations: laziness, poverty, the abandonment of everything. . . . Laziness is the effect of pride; work is a consequence of vanity" (19:9:561). Historical events and social phenomena are difficult to understand because they must be seen as complex totalities, wholes that are composed of various constituent elements whose different proportions affect the whole: women, attitudes toward work, civilization, liberty. By enumerating the different components, Montesquieu attempts to explain why ultimate differences may spring from among apparent similarities.

Mores are spiritual in the sense of not being physical or tangible, and invisible in the sense that they are difficult to isolate and observe. Not surprisingly, they have a more complex impact than physical causes. Susceptible to numerous combinations, "moral qualities produce different effects depending on the other qualities they are attached to" (19:9:561). A nation's mores are never unalloyed: "the diverse characteristics of a nation are mixtures of vice and virtue, of good and bad qualities" (19:10:562). Mores should be distinguished from laws although they are just as powerful. Laws are conscious creations of men, mores their unconscious behavior and thoughts: "Mores and manners are those usages that the law has not established, or could not establish, or did not try to establish" (19:16:566). Laws and mores should not be confused: "it is bad politics to change through laws what should be changed through manners" (19:14:564). To prove the limitations of the law and the necessity of working through the mores to change the deep-seated habits of a people, Montesquieu cites the example of Peter the Great. As czar he tried to westernize Russia very rapidly early in the eighteenth century. He failed because he scorned the old Russian customs. Despite Peter's disregard for their deep and tenacious roots, those ingrained habits inspired a fierce resistance to his reforms and in the end thwarted him completely.

Two sentences comprise the whole of chapter 15. They point to the unifying vision of Montesquieu who is seeking the connections between and among diverse phenomena. "Everything is intimately connected: the despotism of the prince fits naturally with the servitude of women, the liberty of women with the spirit of the monarchy" (19:15:565). To illustrate a single point like this in all its complexity and to investigate its deep, invisible causes is the task that Montesquieu has set for himself in attempting to analyze customs and mores and their impact on laws.

After four chapters on China and Chinese customs, Montesquieu presents a vision of what a truly free people would be like. "I spoke in book 11 about a free people. I gave the principles of their constitution. Let us see the effects which should flow from it, the character which has been formed, and the customs which have resulted from it" (19:27:574). He is alluding to an imaginary England, of course. Nonetheless, this utopian vision does serve to articulate some of the ideal manners and customs that Montesquieu believes would be found in a free country. On this high note about the mores of a free nation the first half of *The Spirit of the Laws* comes to a close.

Fourth Part: Books 20–23

Economics is the topic of this fourth part. In preceding books, especially in the last section, Montesquieu touched upon this subject. There, however, his remarks were largely marginal; here they constitute the essense of these four books as he attempts to analyze the broadest implications of commerce and what we might call its symbolic value as human behavior.[8] Right at the outset he states that commerce implies "easy living" (*les moeurs douces*) and that it naturally leads to peace (20:1). Recalling his earlier correlation of governmental forms, principles, and motivations with the spirit of a nation, Montesquieu believes that differing attitudes regarding commerce stem from different political systems and vice versa. Monarchy favors the production of luxury goods while the republic leans to a more frugal economy based on real market needs. Politics affect economics by determining the spirit behind both: "in a nation in servitude, people work more to maintain [what they have] than to acquire. In a free nation, they work more to acquire than to maintain" (20:5:588). By extension, democracy encourages entrepreneurship and risk taking while under a monarchy business is geared to holding on to what it already has. England is cited as the chief example of a country that "has always subordinated political to commercial interests" (20:7:590).

At the level of international commerce, Montesquieu favors a complete freedom of trade because it is "competition that sets a just price on commodities and that fixes the true relationships among them" (20:9:591). In order to facilitate trade, especially international trade, banks and other associations of businessmen require a freedom not usu-

ally found in a government by a single ruler (20:10:592). Thus commerce thrives in republics and draws monarchies away from despotism
and toward greater liberty.

After discussing economics in history with specific references to the
island of Rhodes, Xenophanes, and the colonial trade of Spain and
Portugal, Montesquieu moves on to the confusing question of nobility
and commerce. Nobles should not be involved in trade, he says, because
"it is contrary to the spirit of commerce that nobility engage in it under
a monarchy" (20:21:598). In England it was precisely this mercantile
spirit that weakened the throne. Nonetheless, he immediately adds that
France is an exception to the rule. Businessmen (he uses the more general term *négociants*) are not themselves noble but they can become noble. The possibility of acquiring noble status, either through marriage
or by the purchase of a suitable position with ennobling prerogatives
(called venality), was much practiced in eighteenth-century France. In
Montesquieu's view, this encouraged the ambitious and the talented to
acquire enough wealth so they could change social class. Such an opportunity to improve oneself is a major advantage: "I say that men will
exercise their profession better when those who excel in it have the hope
of rising to another" (20:22:598). The related issue of whether a nobleman loses his nobility by engaging in commerce still troubles historians. Simon Schama has most recently claimed, contrary to the
traditional view, that the French nobility was more deeply engaged in
commerce before the French Revolution than after it.[9] His challenge to
the received notion that the aristocracy of the ancien régime intentionally avoided the taint of business finds some support in this chapter even
though Montesquieu's observations are too brief to provide a definitive
answer to this question.

In book 21 the power of commerce is revealed. According to Montesquieu, business has transformed the very physical aspect of the land
and the political fate of nations: "Commerce, sometimes destroyed by
conquerors, sometimes hindered by monarchs, runs about the world,
flees when oppressed, remains where it is allowed to breathe. Today it
rules in places where formerly there was only desert, rocks, and sea; in
places where it formerly ruled, there is now only desert" (20:5:604).
Trade becomes a synonym for exchanges of all types and for all we mean
today by the term "communication." Seen in this perspective, trade is
intimately related to the great events that have made history. "The
history of commerce is the history of communications among peoples.
Their diverse destructions as well as the ebb and flow of populations

and devastations comprise its greatest events" (21:5:604). Montesquieu then examines ancient history from this economic angle. He even goes so far as to impute a commercial motive to the conquests of Alexander the Great: "we cannot doubt that his plan was to establish trade with India through Babylon and the Persian Gulf" (21:8:616). Rome was always a land power and never a naval one like Carthage. Since international trade required a powerful navy, Rome could never have become a commercial empire. Roman genius was military, not mercantile: "Besides, their genius, their glory, their military education, the form of their government all removed them from commerce" (21:14:632). In contrast to the Romans whose "spirit . . . was to not trade" (21:15:633), the Arabs seemed "destined for commerce" (21:16:634) but not for war. Contact with the commercial East eventually introduced luxury into Rome. A major element of Rome's fall as Montesquieu studied it in the *Considerations* was the loss of the republican spirit and the consequent transition to monarchy and despotism. Here he explicitly mentions trade as a factor in that transformation: "this new trading produced luxury, which we have proven is as favorable to the rule by one as it is fatal to government by many; . . . this institution dates from the same time as the fall of the republic" (21:16:635).

Such speculations on the impact of commerce lead to at least two important statements. First, Montesquieu pens a warm and intelligent defense of the Jews, who had long been vilified as the moneylenders and usurers of Europe. He points out their positive contributions to trade and society. He is particularly pleased that they used the economic freedom necessary for international banking and other financial transactions to thwart local tyrants. Thus freedom of commerce marks one step toward greater political liberty. "They invented letters of credit [exchange]. In this manner, commerce escaped violence and persevered everywhere. The richest businessman had only invisible goods that could be sent anywhere and that left no trace anywhere" (21:20:640). And so commerce becomes "philosophical" and plays a role as the adversary of despotism. To complete this encomium of trade as another form of politics, Montesquieu does not hesitate to criticize Christian attitudes on economics, especially the theological teachings that placed serious restrictions on lending money and thus on the ability to capitalize any business enterprise. In passing, he belittles the spurious justifications for persecuting Jews: "When the Jews wanted to become Christians their goods were confiscated and, soon afterwards, they were burned when they did not want to become Christian" (21:20:640).

Second, Montesquieu enthusiastically celebrates the sextant. By allowing ships to navigate on the high seas, this invention of science in the service of commerce opened up the entire world to trade (21:21). In *The Persian Letters* Usbek also praised the sextant as another philosophical tool that furthered the progress of enlightened thought.

Chapter 22 was written many years earlier as an independent piece entitled "Essai sur les richesses d'Espagne" ("Essay on the Wealth of Spain").[10] Included in its entirety here, it finds its rightful place within the larger framework of an extended discussion on economics. In contrast to most of his contemporaries, Montesquieu clearly understood that the sudden influx of gold from the colonies paradoxically decreased Spain's real wealth through oversupply and inflation.

In the following book, 22, he continues to unfold this shrewd and modern understanding of money. For Montesquieu, money does not have an absolute or intrinsic value as it did for most other economists of his time. Rather than recognizing it as a fixed value, he sees it as an arbitrary sign that really serves to fix relations between and among other different objects: "Money [*monnoie*] is a sign that represents the value of all goods. A metal is selected so that the sign will be durable and will never wear out. . . . Just as money [*argent*] is the sign of the value of goods, paper is the sign of the value of money. When the paper is good, it represents money so well that, judging by the effects, there is no difference between them" (22:2:651). This notion of money as sign might sound very ordinary today since we are so accustomed to paper money. We must remember, however, that Montesquieu was writing at a time when everyone still remembered the financial chaos caused by John Law's paper money and when the theories of the Physiocrats still dominated economic thinking. Most people believed that wealth was fixed and resided principally in agriculture, not in commerce or manufacturing. Supply and demand were determined by fairly stable populations and not by taste, desire, or disposable income. In contrast to these old-fashioned notions, Montesquieu is voicing a very modern perception about the nature and function of money. Signs, especially monetary signs, can serve for and replace real objects or values. Readers can easily get lost in this play of signifiers especially in French where *monnoie* means money as an exchange vehicle and *argent* means both money and the precious metal silver. In Montesquieu's interchange and exchange of signs, money becomes silver which becomes paper, that is to say, pure symbol or representation. He realizes that silver is a commodity like other metals while it is simultaneously, as a sign, the basis of a system of exchange and the means of evaluating everything else. However fleetingly, Montesquieu has grasped money as a semiotics and as a metadiscourse. As its precise meaning wavers, *argent* becomes in turn both an element within the monetary system and the organizing principle of that system. At this point economics resembles modern literary criticism which evokes notions of literary economy or exchange, plays games with fleeing signifiers, and capitalizes on the loss of fixed values through delayed or deferred meanings.

While neither a modern literary critic nor an economist, Montesquieu does distinguish (22:3) between "real money," which contains its full value in precious metal, and "ideal money," which can be (de) (re-)valued or otherwise fixed at an arbitrary rate that is different from its true worth. Although the fiscal disaster of Law's banking scheme and stock venture was still fresh in the public's memory, Montesquieu explores and defends the validity of a paper currency. This is surprising since he condemned Law and his system so harshly in *The Persian Letters* and in his *Mes Pensées* (My thoughts). A number of his remarks on paper money can be applied to other fiduciary instruments from stocks through bonds to securities and would still be fairly accurate today.

After considering such various related topics as how letters of credit work (22:10) and fluctuations in Roman currency (22:11, 12, 13), Montesquieu returns to money per se. Since it is a sign of exchange, strictly speaking money cannot be owned: "money, which is the price of things, can be rented but not purchased" (22:19:675). Therefore he rejects the religious interdiction on usury. Lending money at interest or "renting" it is perfectly logical and acceptable. Governments are right to allow interest and religions are wrong to forbid it.

Population as it relates to economics is the subject of book 23. There were no reliable censuses in the eighteenth century even though economic theory related wealth directly to population. Demography was therefore a major concern. For Montesquieu, birthrates are not blind or automatic. Rather, they are linked to a variety of interconnected causes, some of which discourage human reproduction. As is so often the case, his favorite example is Rome, where a steadily decreasing birthrate indicated a profound social malaise and announced the impending fall. He notes, "But soon even the wisest laws could not reestablish what a dying republic, general anarchy, military government, harsh empire, proud despotism, a weak monarch, and a stupid, idiotic, and superstitious court had successively beaten down" (23:23:708–9). Population is, for Montesquieu, a vote of confidence that citizens take in their government. In this context of wealth and population, chapter 29 on "hospitals" (i.e., workhouses, an early form of public assistance) strikes a note of generous compassion as Montesquieu expresses his own social consciousness. He declares, "A man is not poor because he possesses nothing, but because he is not working" (23:29:712). A man with a skill always has a resource to fall back upon, like a farmer who tills his own land. While recognizing the importance of personal initiative and responsibility, Montesquieu acknowledges that even private charity cannot replace "the obligation of the state which owes all its citizens a certain subsistence: food, clothing, and a living that is not contrary to good health" (23:29:712). Such comments reveal Montesquieu's real humanity, his sense of human solidarity, and his conviction that the state and the citizen each contribute to the other's welfare.

Fifth Part: Books 24–26

Although this section is small, its subject is large: religion. As a *philosophe*, Montesquieu often found himself opposing the Catholic church's teachings. Knowing that religion could be a dangerous topic, Montesquieu was usually careful to phrase his disagreement in the most innocent way possible. However, such prudence was very difficult to practice in this section where he proposed to examine religion from a purely rationalistic perspective. As he apologetically and somewhat duplicitiously words it, he is seeking "among the false religions those that are most inclined to society's good" (24:1:714).

He begins as the champion of all religions. He refutes Pierre Bayle's defense of atheism by saying that religion remains "the only brake on those who do not fear human laws" (24:2:715). Later he says that even a false religion is the best guarantee we have of men's honesty (24:12). Since it has upheld the right of governments to rule and defended human rights in wartime (24:3), the Christian religion is antithetical to despotism. Consequently he can claim that "Christianity, which seems to have no object other than happiness in the next life, still works toward our happiness in this one" (24:3:716).

Nevertheless, Montesquieu's analytic eye subjects religion to the same critical scrutiny as other phenomena. He recognizes that independence and freedom are found more frequently among Protestants than Catholics. Since Protestantism was more firmly entrenched in northern Europe and Catholicism in the south, the geographical distribution of religions that favor or discourage political freedom coincides with his theory of climates: "The people of the north have had and always will have a spirit of independence and liberty that those in the south do not have; a religion that has no visible leader is better suited to this independence of climate than a religion that does have one" (24:5:718). Never a zealot in theological matters, Montesquieu states that the purpose of both religion and civil government is to "make men good citizens" (24:14:724). Religion and the state are two forces that shape a people and form the specific *esprit* that characterizes a nation.

Still Montesquieu knows he cannot praise other religions too much. He is walking a tightrope, conceding that other religions are wrong even as he indicates that they contribute to the public weal. Consequently, he produces carefully worded judgments that non-Christian religious leaders such as Confucius and Zeno "drew from their erroneous principles consequences that were not correct but still admirable for their society" (24:19:729). Similarly, he finds that the dogmas of the ancient Persians "were false, but they were very useful" (24:20:730). Obviously, Montesquieu is not discussing religion as a credo but rather as a human phenomenon and as a code of behavior whose impact on society deserves a serious critical analysis.

While book 24 considered religion in itself, book 25 deals with its outward manifestations. Here Montesquieu makes a most significant distinction between tolerating and approving another religion. He defends tolerance because repression will only reproduce itself: "It is a principle that any religion that is persecuted persecutes in its turn. For once it throws off its oppression by whatever means, it attacks the religion that persecuted it not as a religion but as tyranny" (25:9:744). Chapter 13, containing the story of a Jew brought before the Inquisition, is a polemic in the tradition of the French *conte philosophique* (philosophical tale engaged in the war of ideas). Entitled the "Très Humble Remontrance aux Inquisiteurs d'Espagne et de Portugal" (Most humble remonstrance to the inquisitors of Spain and Portugal), it is an effective plea for tolerance. Its irony is biting: "You want us to be Christians, and yet you don't want to be Christian yourselves" (25:13:747). In addition to being witty and mordantly sarcastic, the story also voices Montesquieu's passionate commitment to human rights and dignity:

You live in a time when knowledge is stronger than it has ever been, when philosophy has enlightened mens' minds, when the moral of your Gospels has been widely known, when the reciprocal rights of men and the empire of one conscience over another have been well established. If, then, you do not give up your old ways of thinking which (if you are not careful) are but emotional prejudices, all will have to acknowledge that you are incorrigible, incapable of enlightenment or education. A nation that gives authority to men like you would be most unfortunate. . . . You will be cited to prove that these times were uncivilized. The impression you leave will be such that it will curse your times and bring hatred down on your contemporaries. (25:13:748–49)

Ringing with conviction and dignity, these words belong not to the detached analyst and scholar but to the dedicated humanist and libertarian.

As I mentioned at the beginning of this chapter, book 26 provides a capstone to the discussion of religion and forms the natural conclusion to Montesquieu's monumental effort to discuss human behavior, laws, and the spirit that explains them both. He separates the civil from the religious in matters of law: "One cannot decree by divine law what should be decreed by human law, nor can one regulate by human law what should be regulated by the divine" (26:2:751). Today this may appear an ordinary expression of the doctrine of the separation of church and state. However, it was a much more audacious statement in the mid-eighteenth century when religious freedom was largely unknown and when individual rulers decided how their subjects would be permitted to worship.

Given this fundamental principle, Montesquieu can consider issues like divorce and suicide as civil and not religious matters. While separate, civil and religious laws do complement each other. As he puts it, "Religious laws are more sublime, civil laws have a greater reach" (26:9:759). Throughout his treatise, Montesquieu has argued that laws are in themselves insufficient unless they are supported by the mores and the customs, in short by the spirit, of the people: "In a good republic, good mores are what is needed" (26:6:755). Religion plays an important role in determining those mores. Again he condemns the Inquisition because it confuses the religious and the civil arenas that should remain separate and because it violates all the principles of good government: "This tribunal is insufferable under any government. In a monarchy it cannot fail to produce informers and traitors; in a republic, it can only produce dishonest individuals; in a despotism, it is equally destructive" (26:11:761). That final phrase is especially powerful. The abuse of religious authority is as despotic and as tyrannical as that of political power.

Having distinguished the religious and the civil, Montesquieu also separates common law (*loi civile*) from legislated and enacted law (*loi politique*). As Montesquieu made clear in his discussion of the English constitution, such distinctions and separations are important because they prevent the easy usurpation of power. Liberty is protected by laws that no one can violate: "we are therefore free because we live under civil law" (26:20:772). For Montesquieu, liberty does not exist outside society. It is not some natural or primitive state in which men are somehow equal. Liberty is a civil construct, a human creation. Liberty is in the laws that all have to obey.

These oppositions between civil and religious law, between common and political law, repeat the binary distinction that has informed the entire work. In addition to the *lois* that represent the rational side of human behavior, there is the *esprit,* the deeper, unquestioned motivations that underlie and sometimes belie those laws on the surface. Together they comprise *De l'Esprit des lois.*

Sixth Part: Books 28–31

A late addition to the final text, this sixth part is disproportionately long (it comprises about one-third of the whole),[11] and bears little connection to the rest of the work. It is usually considered an oversized appendix clumsily tacked on at the end. Montesquieu experienced similar difficulty in shaping and terminating his *Considerations.* Nonetheless, this final part must have offered him an irresistible temptation to commit to paper the enormous amount of information he had absorbed in his research. This material was surely dear to his heart as a scholar. Part of it echoes his fascination with Rome and the changes in Roman laws on inheritance. The other major theme concerns feudal law. As strange as it may seem, feudal legal practice was a most relevant question in contemporary political debates. Well before the 1740s there had been a continuing controversy about the origin of the French monarchy. One opinion, expressed by Abbé Dubos, held that the French king traced his authority back to Roman law. The other, whose spokesman was Boulainvilliers, argued a "Germanic thesis" that claimed the king was only the first among equals and that he depended for his power on the nobles who surrounded him.[12] Montesquieu especially appreciated Boulainvilliers's theory that the Franks already had the concepts of limited monarchy and aristocratic responsibility. While never definitively resolved, this debate contributed to the decision to convoke the Estates General in 1788, which in turn led to the outbreak of the French

Revolution the following year. In an unforeseen illustration of Montesquieu's theory of intermediary powers limiting the absolute authority of the monarchy, the king called for the support of the nation to institute fiscal and tax reforms since he had neither the will nor the courage to do so alone.

Book 28 argues that Salic law replaced Roman law because it treated Franks better than Romans, thus encouraging the Romans to give up their own laws in favor of the Frankish legal system. In other barbarian tribes, Roman jurisprudence survived intact. Montesquieu also discusses the evolution of trial by combat and the "point of honor," two legal procedures at the heart of Frankish justice.

The short book 29 has two main themes. The first is a comparative study of the similarities and dissimilarities in ancient law. For example, the Greeks and Romans had differing legal views on suicide. The second theme is a comparison between English and French legal systems especially regarding false witness.

In contrast, book 30 offers a long and erudite analysis of Frankish medieval law and its contributions to the establishment of the French monarchy. Montesquieu freely criticizes Abbé Dubos whose colossal argument about Roman law has "feet of clay" (30:23:926) and whose "whole system . . . crumbles from top to bottom" (30:24:928).

The last book continues this discussion of the Franks. One of its main points is the history of how the king was displaced by the mayor of the palace. Montesquieu emphasizes the mixture of heredity and selection in this latter office. The other major subject is an intricate account of feudal rights, of fiefs, vassals, and liege lords, and the interwoven duties, privileges, and prerogatives of the aristocracy.

With this protracted discussion of feudal law and history Montesquieu's monumental work finally ends.

The *Defense*

Even though the *Laws* was immediately recognized as a masterpiece, a negative reaction against it soon sprang up. It culminated with the book's condemnation by the Catholic church and its insertion on the Index of forbidden readings. As criticism increased in journals edited by both Jesuits and Jansenists (an unusual alliance since they usually were bitter enemies, agreeing on nothing), Montesquieu felt he could no longer maintain his silence and had to defend himself personally in print. His "La Défense de l'*Esprit des Lois*" (Defense of "The Spirit of the Laws") appeared in 1750.

From the point of view of ideas, the *Defense* is disappointing. Montesquieu advances no new arguments and he fails to reformulate or sharpen his most important ideas. Even worse, he adapts a conciliatory tone, and he quibbles about minor details. His strategy seems to be to move the whole debate away from the really controversial and dangerous areas toward issues where disagreement would be permissible.

All in all, the *Defense* misses the mark. Montesquieu is unable to deflect the principal objection that he has mounted a powerful albeit indirect attack against Christianity. Quite simply, he has investigated religion as just one of a number of human behaviors. Furthermore, he has given it second place, behind civil government, in the task of ruling men. Of course, Montesquieu never said any of this openly. But his attitude can be read between the lines and in the implications both of his material and his methodology. By refusing to engage his detractors on this basic issue, Montesquieu implicitly admits that they were correct.

Despite the lukewarm *Defense, The Spirit of the Laws* continued to be hailed as Montesquieu's masterpiece and even as the single most important book of the eighteenth century. It was truly a seminal work that powerfully influenced for close to two centuries all those who came afterwards.

Chapter Six
Minor Works

Finding a way to discuss Montesquieu's numerous other works poses some real methodological problems. Most of them are short and deal with diverse topics so that a common, unifying theme is missing. Most do not lend themselves to summary because their value is more often in the details than in the whole. Most did not see print until long after they were written; many, in fact, were not even published during the author's lifetime. It is not without cause that these works are called "minor." There is no doubt that they lack the defining imprint of Montesquieu's genius. Nonetheless, secondary though they are, these writings deserve some attention, however brief.

To organize my discussion, I propose dividing these minor works into groups according to their subject matter or presentational devices. This categorization, although crude, does reveal significant affinities among the texts grouped together. The thoughts and themes that recur in the minor mode demonstrate the consistency of Montesquieu's intellectual interests across the years and counterpoint their more expert orchestration in his other, more acclaimed publications.

Compilations and Local Topics

These two subjects belong together because, frankly speaking, they contain the least interesting of Montesquieu's minor works. In the eighteenth century, long before the age of Xerox, serious researchers copied out by hand long passages from the books they were studying. A meticulous and well-disciplined scholar, Montesquieu kept a number of such volumes in which he recorded interesting facts picked up in his readings. Sometimes he would copy out passages in their entirety, while at other times he would include only an analysis, a résumé, a judgment, or a reaction. Most of these compilations have been lost. However, his *Geographica* as well as a more diverse collection entitled *Spicilège* have survived. As the title indicates, the former volume concentrates on geography. The lost volumes had titles like *Politica* (Politics), *Juridica* (Law), *Mythologica et antiquitates* (Mythology and Antiquity), *Anatomica* (Anatomy), *Historica Universalis* (World History), and *Commerce* (Commerce), indications of Montesquieu's broad reading and study. The *Spicilège,* a French term based on its Latin cognate meaning "harvest" or "gleanings," was less precise in its focus. While largely composed of excerpts taken from journals or newspapers, it also included Montesquieu's personal reflections in the spirit of commonplace books of his epoch. When he records anecdotes, they are much in the same style as those in his travel notebooks: he notes the underside or the inside of political life, such as the actions of state turning on personal considerations.

As a landowner and wine producer in the Bordeaux area, Montesquieu also wrote on topics of local interest. His "Questionnaire sur la culture de la vigne en Guyenne" (Questionnaire on cultivating vineyards in Guyenne) deals with wine production while his "Mémoire contre l'arrêt du conseil du 27 février 1725" (Memoir against the administrative decision of 27 February 1725) marks his opposition to a decree that forbade the planting of new vineyards. He wrote funeral tributes, called *éloge* in French, for the duc de la Force and the maréchal de Berwick. Something like long obituaries, these rhetorical compositions joined personal feelings with a public statement about a prominent individual who had just died. Montesquieu also committed to paper some "Souvenirs de la cour de Stanislas Leczinski" (Memories of the court of Stanislas) about his visit to the ex-king of Poland's court in Lunéville. Finally, there are official statements or "reception" discourses that Montesquieu read when he was inducted into the Bordeaux Académie and the Académie Française.

Politics and Philosophy

This large group contains many apparently disparate works that share an analytic approach to major social and/or political issues. This is the kind of material Montesquieu meditated upon throughout his life. Here are found many of his principal ideas as they are being worked out, thoughts that have not yet reached their final expression or the form under which they will become best known.

The "Réflexions sur le caractère de quelques princes" (Reflections on the character of some princes) is a fragment from a larger, unfinished historical work. Imitating Plutarch's *Parallel Lives,* each section compares and contrasts two famous monarchs. Choices range over all Europe and even include a pair of popes. In one example Montesquieu compares Charles the Bold and Charles the soldier-king of Sweden, a legend even before his death in 1718 and the subject of one of Voltaire's histories: "Charles XII, king of Sweden, and Charles, the last duke of Burgundy: the same courage, the same confidence, the same ambition, the same fearlessness, the same successes, the same misfortunes, and the same end."[1] Doubtless anecdotal and narrative history did not fully satisfy Montesquieu who moved on to search for underlying causes and determining principles in his subsequent work.

Montesquieu delivered a "Discours sur l'équité" (Discourse on justice) on 12 November 1725 when the Bordeaux law court opened its session. It was not published until 1771. For a time thereafter it was sold at the session's opening to remind everyone concerned of the responsibility of magistrates in assuring that justice be done. Oratorical in the eighteenth-century style, this speech provides an eloquent statement of how laws should be enforced: "I will speak only of those incidentals which can determine whether justice will be more or less prevalent. Justice must be enlightened; it must be prompt; justice must not be harsh, and finally it has to be universal" (*Oeuvres Complètes,* 184d). These four essential qualities of justice are as appropriate today as they were then. In his conclusion Montesquieu apostrophizes lawyers, exhorting them to practice their profession virtuously. The continuous return to an ideal of civic virtue marks all of his thinking.

This same concern with civic and social virtue is found in "De la considération et de la réputation" (On public esteem and reputation) which was read on 25 August 1725 (published in 1891). Montesquieu is convinced that intangible moral factors such as reputation produce the sense of community that society needs if it is to be viable: "Public esteem contributes much more to our happiness than birth, wealth, position, honors; I do not know any sadder role in society than that of a rich lord without merit, who is never treated but in phrases marked with respect instead of those natural and heartfelt expressions [traits] that bring out the public esteem" (*Oeuvres complètes,* 182d). Montesquieu's phrase is circular, complete in itself, offering no opening for disagreement. Between its identical opening and closing terms ("public esteem"), it leads us through a detailed enumeration ("birth, wealth, position, honors") illustrating the concept more than explaining it. Lost unfortunately in translation is the rhetorical antithesis that contrasts "treated with respect" ("traité avec respect") with "natural and heartfelt expressions" ("traits naifs et délicats"). Montesquieu's syntax carries a substantial part of his argument. He is both a writer and a thinker. He expresses himself as much in his words as in his style, as much in what his words say as in how they are arranged to say it.

The "Essai touchant les lois naturelles et la distinction du juste et de l'injuste" (Essay on natural laws) remained unpublished until André Masson's edition in 1951–55. In it Montesquieu attempts to answer the age-old question whether laws are God-given or whether they are of human origin. He defends the latter point of view. Laws are needed to check men's passions. A first argument advances the theory that laws are implied both by God's goodness and by man's need for cooperation and mutual aid: "What we want others to do to us, that is the desire that inspires us with the love of ourselves; let us do the same for others, that is the advice this love give us. . . . All men will think only of helping each other. That will comprise a single family. . . . the earth will become a paradise" (*Oeuvres complètes,* 178–79). This entire passage echoes religious concepts and terms. A second argument invokes societal norms that transcend private values: "Just and unjust, virtue and vice are no longer things that depend on the whim of legislators. They are fixed and as distinct as the good and evil they cause in society. In a word, any law without which society could not exist becomes by that fact alone a divine Law" (*Oeuvres complètes,* 180d).

A related work, "Traité des devoirs" (Treatise on duty, 1725), has been lost. Although it is known only through some scribe's résumé, we recognize the ideas even in the paraphrase. "The author, in chapters four and five, demonstrates that justice does not depend on human laws, that it is founded on the existence and social nature of reasonable beings, and not on the particular intentions or desires of these beings" (*Oeuvres complètes,* 181d). Montesquieu's opposition to Hobbes is specifically mentioned.

"De la politique" (On politics) appears to be a couple of chapters taken out of the lost treatise on duty just mentioned. Two points deserve discussion. First, Montesquieu is preparing a thought that will reach its ultimate illustration and expression in his history of Rome. It touches on the unpredictable effects of minor causes: "Most results are effected in ways that are so singular or depend on such imperceptible or distant causes that one can scarcely foresee them" (*Oeuvres complètes,* 172). Already Montesquieu is distancing himself from the mind-set that attributed all significant events to kings and generals, the "great man" theory of historiography. A complementary principle involves deep causes and articulates the essential point in Montesquieu's historical determinism. Given the underlying factors, one outcome is inevitable. Appearances or other superficial causes that seem to announce a different denouement are, in fact, insignificant in comparison with those deeper motivations: "that the general spirit, the events, the situations, and the respective interests were in such a state that this effect had to result from it, no matter what cause, what power was in operation" (*Oeuvres complètes*, 173c). Second, he articulates more clearly here than elsewhere what he means by the "spirit" or the "character" of a people:

In all societies, which are nothing but spiritual unions, a common character is formed. This universal soul takes on a way of thinking that is the result of a chain of infinite causes that multiply and interact from century to century. Once the tone is given and takes root, it alone governs. All that sovereigns, magistrates, and peoples can do or imagine is related to this tone, whether they shock it or follow it. This tone dominates [a society] until its total destruction. (*Oeuvres complètes*, 173c).

This tone defines the deep-seated and hidden causes. This is the "spirit" behind legal codes and practices that Montesquieu will uncover in his *The Spirit of The Laws.*

Even in this early text Montesquieu has formulated two ideas critical to all his subsequent writings. But they are not immutable, fixed here once and for all. Rather, they will change continuously in their details. As they are borrowed, applied, and adjusted to various and changing subject matters, they will appear in multiple versions and expressions that constitute the record of Montesquieu's unflagging search for the constant principles behind the complexities of human experience.

"Reflexions sur la monarchie universelle en Europe" (Reflections on universal monarchy in Europe, written about 1727, not published until 1891) focuses on the importance of a strong ruler, especially in military matters, while it provides a political and historical overview of most European and a few Asian countries. Montesquieu discusses issues like the balance of power (what in the twentieth century would be known as the doctrine of mutually assured destruction), which he had already touched on in *The Persian Letters*: "they gain nothing that way except mutual self-destruction. Each of the monarchs has at the ready all the weapons they would need if their peoples were in danger of being exterminated, and we call peace this state of everyone striving against everyone else" (*Oeuvres complètes*, 197c). He observes how Spain's gold, imported from the New World, precipitated her decline: "there was an internal, physical vice in the nature of these riches that increased every day and made them useless. There is no one who does not know that gold and silver are merely fictitious or conventional riches. . . . The Spaniards' misfortune was that by the conquest of Mexico and Peru they abandoned real and natural riches in order to have the fictitious ones that degenerated all by themselves" (*Oeuvres complètes,* 195d). He foretells what will become the principal theme of his study of the rise and fall of Rome: "it happens that a state that appears victorious outside ruins itself inside . . . and decline begins especially in the time of those greatest successes that can be maintained only by violent means" (*Oeuvres complètes,* 193a).

The "Essay on the Wealth of Spain," written about 1728 and published in 1910, demonstrates one compositional trait found throughout Montesquieu: borrowing. Montesquieu reuses material from this essay both in his "Reflexions sur la monarchie universelle en Europe" and in *The Spirit of the Laws.* Ideas reoccur while their formulation and context vary. The same considerations return in print as Montesquieu turns these complex phenomena over in his mind. In nine articles, Montesquieu explains how the colonies in the New World ruined the mother country. They sent back so much gold that this sudden influx of wealth disrupted normal commerce and destroyed Spain's economic health. Montesquieu understands that gold is not intrinsically valuable but rather an economic convention, nothing more than an arbitrary sign of wealth. Unlike real riches, which consist of manufactured goods and foodstuffs, false wealth like gold and silver is "a fictional usuage" (*Oeuvres complètes,* 208b) because it itself does not produce or create anything of value. A precapitalist, Montesquieu underestimated money's productive possibilities, like most eighteenth-century economic thinkers who considered farming the prime source of wealth. He was astute enough, however, to contrast the actual production of the land, which he regarded as real wealth, to plunder or booty that was unhealthy and pernicious both socially and economically. For Montesquieu, economic and political danger lies in confusing real and fictional riches: "many consider these metals to be the cause of the power of those states, although they are nothing but the sign of it" (*Oeuvres complètes,* 210c). Montesquieu remembers that one major cause of Rome's fall was precisely the inflation that followed the loot back from the wars, an economic disaster that had significant moral repercussions.

The "Essai sur les causes qui peuvent affecter les esprits et les caractères" (Essay on the causes that can affect mind and character) was not published until 1892. Its date of composition is unknown but it surely belongs to the same period as *The Spirit of the Laws* (1748), to which it is closely related.[2] The discussion centers on analyzing how various peoples of the same human race came to have different ways of behaving and living. By giving equal weight to the physical and the moral, this essay clearly establishes an equilibrium that is often forgotten when Montesquieu's so-called historical determinism or his ideas on climate are criticized: "there is, in every nation, a general character. . . . It is produced in two ways: by physical causes that depend on the climate . . . ; and by moral causes, which are a combination of laws, religion, mores, and social customs" (*Oeuvres complètes,* 492c). From these factors come the spirit of a nation, its distinctive genius, its defining character. While attempting to be as scientific as possible in discussing the physical aspects of the human body, Montesquieu also uses some evocative metaphors. The central nervous system is compared to a musical instrument whose strings vibrate; later it is likened to a spider's web: "The soul [i.e., what we would call the central nervous system] is, in our body, like a spider in its web. This spider cannot move without vibrating at least one of its strands that are extended into the distance, and similarly, we cannot shake one of these strands without moving it" (*Oeuvres complètes,* 489b).

The "Memoire sur la Constitution" (Memoir on the Constitution, 1753) articulates clearly and courageously Montesquieu's opinion on the struggle between Jesuits and Jansenists that dated back at least 100 years and continued until the suppression of the Jesuit order in France in 1762. In the mid-seventeenth century, Nicole and some other hermits, known as the *solitaires* of Port-Royal, seconded by Pascal and exerting an influence on Racine, opposed the pope who had condemned the Dutch bishop Jansénius and his teachings on sanctifying grace as heretical. In 1713, the papal bull *Unigenitus,* better known as the Constitution, again condemned Jansenism by refuting a recent defense written by Père Quesnel. It failed, however, to end the schism or to put a stop to the quarrel. In 1749 the long-smoldering conflict burst into new flame when the archbishop of Paris, Christophe de Beaumont, instructed his priests to deny the sacraments to anyone who had not accepted the Constitution of 1713. In March 1752 the curate of Saint Etienne-du-Mont in Paris refused the last rites to a dying Jansenist. The Parlement, which was heavily Jansenist in its sympathies, had the curate arrested. In May 1753 the king exiled Parlement and the magistrates were not allowed to return to Paris until October. Montesquieu wrote this memoir to the king in the heat of a burning political and religious conflict.

He begins by distinguishing between what he calls internal tolerance, which touches on one's private beliefs, and external tolerance, which concerns the coexistence of differing beliefs. Society's obligation is to protect by law this diversity of opinion among its citizens. The danger lies in confusing the private and the public. One may have a personal belief, but no one has the right to impose that belief on others: "My conscience tells me to not approve internally those who disagree with me; but my conscience also tells me that there are situations when my duty is to tolerate them externally" (*Oeuvres complètes*, 843d). Montesquieu separates church from state, the individual's private convictions from his public tolerance of others. He argues that different opinions in religious matters should not intrude into the political sphere: "the prince's conscience does not oblige him to be informed about those issues over which the theologians themselves are arguing" (*Oeuvres complètes*, 844b). Not really interested in the religious issue per se that was at the origin of all these troubles, Montesquieu calls for a suspension of any further discussion until tempers cool and all is forgotten. He even proposes to label as a "disturber of the peace" anyone who would try to keep the squabble alive. Here, as elsewhere, Montesquieu has the courage to raise a calm and rational voice amid the din of factionalism and fanaticism.

Letters and Dialogues

In this group I place three works that have a strong political content and that are presented in the fictionalized form of either letters or dialogue. The dialogue was used in the eighteenth century much as the newspaper editorial or the op-ed page is today. As a recognized literary genre it dates back to Plato and was given a renewed vigor in eighteenth-century France by such writers as Saint-Evremond and Fontenelle. Montesquieu observes the usual conventions. To real figures plucked from classical Greece or Rome he ascribes invented opinions that are nonetheless plausible in their mouths and that distance the author from any controversy they might provoke. Today these pseudo–re-creations seem cold and lifeless. Modern readers fail to appreciate the subtlety required to blend past and present convincingly or to create some satisfying action in these parlous encounters. Despite their obvious shortcomings, these works are worth some mention for their political content.

As depicted in the "Dialogue entre Xantippe et Xénocrate" (Dialogue of Xantippes to Xenocrates, 1723, published in 1745), Xantippes is modest in demeanor but committed to a high ideal of civic virtue and liberty. Exiled from his native Sparta, he became a Carthagenian general and defeated the Romans in the First Punic war. Because Rome "demanded something else after the glory of victory and tried to be unjust because it had been successful" (*Oeuvres complètes*, 153c), Xantippes felt it his duty to oppose them: "Is not every Spartan born the protector of everyone's liberty?" (*Oeuvres complètes*, 153d). Even though he is a hero, Xantippes remains subservient to the rule of law: "Scrupulous observance of the law is an honor among us" (*Oeuvres complètes*, 154c). This entire anecdote is designed to promote the ideals of honor and duty and to instill principles of civic behavior.

The "Lettres de Xénocrate à Phérès" (Letters of Xenocrates to Pheres, 1723, published in 1892) are really no more than a litany of *maximes* that describe Alcamene who is transparently Philippe d'Orléans, the regent from 1715 to 1723. A lapidary quality and the use of understatement make this portrait highly artificial, as a typical sentence indicates: "Alcamene has turned away few women; but there are precious few who can boast that he held them in his esteem" (*Oeuvres complètes*, 155c). Philippe was, in fact, a compulsive womanizer whose notorious debauchery set the licentious tone of the Regency period. Besides the licentious and the erotic, there are political issues to be raised. And Montesquieu knows how to be critical. He calls the financial system of John Law a "dream" and the "cause of widespread misery" (*Oeuvres complètes*, 155d). He mocks the regent's prime minister, Cardinal Dubois, as "a man of no birth" whose ambition was seconded by luck and not by skill or merit.

Montesquieu probably read his "Dialogue de Sylla et d'Eucrate" (Dialogue between Sylla and Eucrates) at the Entresol between 1724 and 1728. Sylla explains his conduct during the Civil War in Rome and why he later resigned his powers as dictator in 79 B.C.. Despite his bloody proscriptions, Sylla claims to have restored liberty to the Romans. The people were on the point of making themselves slaves in their blind struggle to overwhelm the Senate. The price of liberty was high but had to be paid since the gods have "attached as many sorrows to liberty as they have to servitude" (*Oeuvres complètes*, 157d). Throughout the dialogue Sylla is terribly conscious of his "glory." He explains

that his exceptional nature rejected the mediocre task of daily government and accepted only the extraordinary challenge of conquest. He
opposed Marius because the latter was a low-born commoner. His pa-
trician pride rebelled against Marius's attempt to level the leading families. As a whole this dialogue is confusing because it seems to make the
tyrant Sylla a hero. The members of the Entresol gave it a cool reception, a reaction that most readers since have shared.

Art and Science

In 1753 D'Alembert asked Montesquieu to write an article on taste
for the *Encyclopédie* that he was then editing with Diderot. Although
never finished, it appeared posthumously in 1757 in volume 7 under
the title "Goût" (Taste). Montesquieu defines taste as the "advantage
of discovering with finesse and speed the measure of pleasure that each
thing should give men" (*Oeuvres complètes*, 845a). Thus, by his own
definition, he is led to examine the various sources of pleasure, including curiosity, order, variety, symmetry, and surprise. He criticizes, for
example, too much recourse to contrast and antithesis: "A turn of the
phrase that is always uniform and always the same is extremely displeas-
ing; that perpetual contrast becomes symmetry, and the ever sought-
after opposition becomes uniformity. . . . you see words in opposition,
but opposed in the same manner" (*Oeuvres complètes*, 847d). Unfortunately, Montesquieu did not always take his own advice. His style,
heavily dependent on symmetrically arranged contrasts, frequently falls
into the monotony he correctly denounces here. He attempts to analyze
the *je ne sais quoi*, the unknown, the ineffable ingredient that gradually
came to be a fundamental part of eighteenth-century aesthetics. He sees
this much-desired "indescribable something" in the element of surprise
or in the unexpected: "Paul Veronese promises a lot and repays all that
he promises. Raphael and Correggio promise little and repay a lot. And
that is even more pleasing" (*Oeuvres complètes*, 849c). Montesquieu also
finds beauty and aesthetic pleasure in the *négligé* which is both a characteristic of art and a seductive bit of female clothing: "Nothing pleases
us so much in dress as that neglect or even that disorder which hides
from us all the care that neatness has not required" (*Oeuvres complètes*,
849d). In addition, he recognizes the paradox inherent in the concept
of sophistication and perfection: "So grace can not be acquired: to have
it, you must be a natural. But how can you work at being natural?"
(*Oeuvres complètes*, 849d). Finally, like every true classical writer, he

addresses the issue of observing or breaking the rules: "taste reveals to us those instances when art should command and those when it should submit" (*Oeuvres complètes*, 851c). As these citations have quite obviously shown, Montesquieu does not answer the question of what taste is. Rather he circles around the problem, but in so doing he offers a number of insights into what the eighteenth century would recognize as good taste.

A short essay usually placed with the travel writings can be discussed with profit here. "De la manière gothique" (On the gothic style, published in 1896) was inspired by his trip to Italy and by seeing the great paintings of the Italian Renaissance. By "gothic" Montesquieu means decadent. In art as in history and in all human affairs, there is an inevitable rhythm of rise and fall: "These different stages through which art passes from its birth to its perfection, and from its perfection to its decline, can be seen, in the former case, in the monuments we have from the last century when sculpture and painting were renewed up to Raphael and Michelangelo; and, in the latter, in the Greek and Latin monuments after the great masters of Greece up to the late Roman empire" (*Oeuvres complètes*, 364a). Culture plays an important role in determining what art is and how we judge it. Different nations have produced different kinds of art because their cultures have privileged different values. For example, "Indians [i.e., people from India] have such an extreme loathing for nudity that, even today, in everything they paint, they are ignorant of drawing. How can they paint a body, when they know nothing of its proportions?" (*Oeuvres complètes*, 364d). One of these influential cultural forces is religion. Here Montesquieu pinpoints the artistically negative impact of sects like the Puritans or the Methodists who came close to considering any religious art idolatrous: "The devotions that the Catholic religion allows to be paid to images has contributed heavily to renew, among us, the art that this same sect had nourished among the Greeks. And, if the Protestant religion had won out in Europe, how many beautiful works of art would we have been deprived of?" (*Oeuvres complètes*, 365b). Montesquieu articulated a similar idea in his travel notebooks where he indicated how much he appreciated the aesthetic contribution of the church of Rome despite his general disagreement with its position in matters of politics.

Under this same heading along with art I would include some writings that have a definite scientific bent, beginning with a discourse, read to the Bordeaux Académie in 1725, "on the motives that should encourage our interest in science." In typical eighteenth-century fashion

Montesquieu runs the arts and sciences together and claims that interest in them is a mark of civilization ("grandes nations"), while a lack of interest indicates primitivism ("peuples sauvages"). Science is useful because it destroys harmful prejudices; the pleasure we derive from its study helps us to forget our mortality. Shifting to the arts, Montesquieu warns us that style is not always a reliable indicator of intrinsic worth: "often we have said gravely infantile things; often we have said in a playful manner some very serious truths" (*Oeuvres complètes,* 188d).

Science was one of Montesquieu's lifelong preoccupations. To indicate, however inadequately, the extent of this interest, I simply list here the titles of the scientific papers he presented to the Bordeaux Académie or published separately.

The Cause of Echoes (1 May 1718)

The Function of the Renal Glands (25 August 1718)

Physical History of the Earth (published in the *Mercure de France,* January 1719)

The Cause of Weight in Bodies (1 May 1720)

The Cause of Transparency in Bodies (25 August 1720)

Observations on Natural History (16 and 20 November 1721)

Although his own scientific activity diminished as time went on, Montesquieu did try to encourage the scientific research of others through the network of provincial and international academies and their correspondences.

Fiction

This final group includes several short works of fiction done in the spirit and style of *The Persian Letters.* All are set in an oriental decor that serves principally to distance and disguise the content. Montesquieu was exceptionally prudent in restricting the distribution (in manuscript copies) and delaying publication of these works. This prudence was reinforced by the choice of a setting far from France and convenient for denying any provocation that the texts themselves might elicit. All are erotic ("pornographic" would be too strong a judgment) in the eighteenth-century style. Descriptions are never precise. Rather, they are willfully ambiguous, playing with suggestive connotations that lie just beyond reach. Montesquieu's erotic is never visceral or visual; it is cerebral. Unfortunately, that is not what we consider erotic. Nevertheless, we should not underestimate the effectiveness or the impact of such fiction for an eighteenth-century reader, especially one who might have known that the author was a well-established scholar, a socially prominent aristocrat, and a magistrate. Taste in the erotic changes quickly, as do the standards by which it is judged. Nevertheless, these fictions also contain some politically or socially significant material. Fiction is not a total stranger to the polemics informed by political ideas and social criticism, as the example of *The Persian Letters* demonstrates so convincingly.

The *Histoire véritable* (True story) was composed between 1723 and 1738 and was not published during Montesquieu's lifetime. It combines a picaresque plot with an oriental setting. Belief in reincarnation caused quite a stir in France when it was first introduced from the Far East in the eighteenth century. The narrator-hero tells of the reincarnations that made him a wanderer through various beings and various social classes: he was at different times an elephant, a black eunuch, a horse, a woman, and a rake. He delivers ironic commentaries on all his experiences. A cow in Egypt, he is found one day by priests who mistake him for the god Apis and adore him: "I have, since becoming a man again, made large fortunes without having earned them any more than that time" (*Oeuvres complètes,* 498b). An elephant, he learns how captive beasts enjoy breaking and training wild ones: "Those who live in slavery are just as much the enemies of another's liberty as are those who rule with more power" (*Oeuvres complètes,* 498c). Later he becomes "the most fashionable man of [his] time" by cheating at cards. He rises to such an elevated rank even though he admits that he "was a man of importance although I had neither position, nor worth, nor birth, nor wit, nor honesty, nor education" (*Oeuvres complètes,* 500a).

Although these thrusts are all pointed, they lack emotional impact. The style is too light. The bitter social criticism this material could have produced remains in the end a semisweet game of words. After numerous transmigrations, this picaro-soul becomes a philosopher. Advising his king, he explains that one frivolous activity, theatergoing, has replaced a more serious one, business, in the mores of the people: "These things, so useless in other days, have become important for [the people]. . . . You are shocking its taste, that taste which is liberty. Sire, a corrupted people busies itself with what amuses a virtuous one" (*Oeuvres complètes,* 511c). Jean-Jacques Rousseau will later pick up on this correlation between social decay and the theater and make that issue one of the dividing points between eighteenth-century neoclassicism and romanticism. The narrator of the story has also learned the lesson that informs Montesquieu's history of Rome: "When nations are prosperous, they always become corrupt. Luxury, pleasure, and softness attack everyone's soul" (*Oeuvres complètes,* 510d). Nonetheless, he observes that adversity can bring out the best in men: "But, when a nation experiences great calamities, virtue has a habit of reappearing, the social mores get stronger, men's souls become more courageous and acquire more grandeur" (*Oeuvres complètes,* 511a). Such ideas on the moral weight of a people and the principles of rise and fall are not just pieces of a harmless fiction. On the contrary, they bear testimony to Montesquieu's conviction that the deepest underlying principles of human behavior can be illustrated with a machine metaphor of weight and counterweight just as those same principles can be effectively discussed through the medium of fiction.

Arsace et Isménie (Arsace and Isménie, 1742; published in 1783) is a contrived story of love and politics set in an imaginary Eastern kingdom.[3] An unknown young man saves the kingdom of Bactria from invasion. Aspar, first eunuch and prime minister of Queen Isménie, recognizes the young man's worth and asks him to tell his life story.

The young man's name is Arsace. He tells how the king of his native Media wanted him to abandon his wife, Ardasire, whom he loved, in order to marry the king's daughter. Rather than part, Arsace and Ardasire flee. After living for a time in complete happiness, Arsace longs to do glorious deeds and thus be worthy of his father. He therefore goes to the royal court of Margiane and performs heroic exploits. Rumor has it that the Margiane princess is in love with him, too. A jealous Ardasire kidnaps Arsace, forces him to dress like a woman, and keeps him prisoner in her harem to break his pride. Arsace believes, however, that he has been abducted by the Margiane princess. When he is finally allowed into the presence of his captor, she is veiled. Still her beauty seduces him. Unable to forget his dear Ardasire, he is equally unable to resist this other mysteriously attractive woman. In a climactic confrontation, he almost succeeds in consummating an infidelity that is really not one! Shortly thereafter, Ardasire reveals her true identity. After Arsace recovers from his surprise, she chastises him and falls into his arms.

Now they are blissfully living in Sagdiane. The local tyrant learns of Ardasire's beauty and desires her. He summons her to his court. Arsace disguises himself as a woman and takes her place in the harem. When, in another climactic scene the tyrant's passion for the supposed Ardasire

reaches its peak, Arsace slays him. He returns to Ardasire's palace only
to find her dying. Thinking that he had deserted her, she has committed suicide.

Arsace's story ended, Aspar remembers that years ago, "for reasons
of state," he had sent the king's daughter, Isménie, to Media where she
had married Arsace under the name Ardasire. In secret and throughout
all their ordeals, he had watched over the couple. He had even supplied
them with money when they were in financial need without their sus-
pecting it. Now Aspar reveals to the Bactrians that their former king
had fathered twin daughters. The one who had inherited the throne
died unexpectedly and so he recalled Ardasire from her exile. The sub-
stitution was not noticed. Aspar presents Arsace at court where the
queen, formerly Ardasire and now Isménie, recognizes her husband. He
is acclaimed king. The story ends with pious anecdotes concerning the
new king's wise behavior and with his pronouncements of how one
should rule.

My rather long summary shows how artificial this story is. Its value,
however, lies not in the plot but rather in the gentle eroticism of certain
situations and the political issues indirectly invoked. Here, for example, is the scene in which Arsace is torn between the memory of Ardasire and the attraction of the woman he does not yet recognize as his
wife:

She threw herself at me and hugged me in her arms. Suddenly the room
became dark, her veil opened; she gave me a kiss. I was completely beside
myself. A sudden flame coursed through my veins and heated my senses. . . .
Already I had lifted my hands to her breasts, running them rapidly all over
her; love showed itself in this frenzy; it rushed to its victory; one moment more
and Ardasire would be able to resist no longer. Suddenly she made one last
effort. She was helped, she slipped away from me, and I lost her. (*Oeuvres
complètes*, 518d)

Political themes appear directly and indirectly throughout the story.
The eunuch is a competent minister, but still one who works in secret
beyond the control of any law or other authority. The tyrant's ag-
gressiveness is directed both at countries and individuals. His desire for
conquest is reflected in his lust for women. One could say that his
politics are sexual. The purity of an isolated life in the country is
contrasted with the dangers of living in society. In addition to such
indirect commentary, there are many political maxims in the pages that

close the story. Arsace, for example, "was convinced that in a state good should flow only through the channel of the laws" (*Oeuvres complètes,* 523d). He knows how to rule because he knows how citizens behave: "He said that being born a subject, he had wished a thousand times to live under a good prince and that his subjects doubtless had the same wish as he did" (*Oeuvres complètes,* 523c).

By itself this story is not at all significant; within the context of Montesquieu's other work, we recognize the same preoccupations expressed in another form.

"Céphise et l'Amour" (Céphise and Cupid, published 1743) is nothing more than a long description of a young woman who steals sleeping Cupid's bow. Céphise clips his wings so that Cupid has to return to Venus whose love makes them grow back. To avenge himself, Cupid makes Céphise the most inconstant of lovers.

This anecdote illustrates well the intellectualized eroticism of Montesquieu's rococo style. His fragile and contorted description means both what it says and something more. It operates on two separate levels, with an elusive, suggested referent that can easily escape notice. While always discreet and elegant on the surface, the hidden subtext deals with sexual "wounds" and phallic arrows. To "die" is a well-known euphemism for sexual climax. In equally ambiguous terms and gestures Cupid "grew tired shooting off his arrows" (*Oeuvres complètes,* 525b). When Cupid's wings are clipped, the heat from Venus's body makes them grow back. "Remain on my breast, don't move," she tells Cupid, "the heat will make it grow again. Can't you see that already it's bigger? Kiss me; it's growing; soon you will have it just as it was before; already I see the tip glowing" (*Oeuvres complètes,* 525d). Without exaggeration and without insisting, the text is double, operating on two levels of meaning. Montesquieu always wanted readers who were intelligent enough to appreciate his intricate and demanding texts regardless of whether they were political or erotic.

"Le Temple de Gnide" (The Temple of Gnidus) was first published in 1725 and reissued in 1743 along with *Céphise et L'Amour.* It is presented as a translation from the Greek, another example of Montesquieu hiding his authorship behind the mask of an editor, compiler, or translator. Composed of seven *chants* or chapters, it is a literary isle of Cythera, a written *fête galante* that corresponds to Watteau's painted versions of idle lovers strolling in a parklike decor. Only indirectly can one discern a political component hidden behind these ornamental decorations: "No one in this city distinguishes between voluptuousness and necessities; all the arts that might trouble a peaceful sleep have been banished; at public expense prizes are given to those who discover a new voluptuousness; the citizens remember only the clowns who amused them and they have forgotten the magistrates who governed them" (*Oeuvres complètes,* 167–68). The unbridled pursuit of pleasure has political implications for society as illustrated by the frivolity and the social upheaval of the Regency that Montesquieu observed at close hand.

The "Voyage à Paphos" (Voyage to Paphos, published in the *Mercure de France* in 1727, republished in 1747) offers a minimal plot that really serves to justify the presence of several lovers and their amorous conversations, all in a pseudo-classical setting of nymphs, gardens, and Venus's pleasure palaces. One passage describing such a palace is worth quoting because it catches a significant aspect of Montesquieu's style: "Who can describe its beauties? No, Melite, I will not undertake it. Your imagination is enough. It will not allow you to let anything escape that art might have invented to create an abode worthy of the Greeks" (*Oeuvres complètes,* 200c). Montesquieu is suggesting that author and reader engage in a communication that precedes and transcends mere words. Both know the code so well that even the most conventional phrase evokes the maximal meaning. Rather than multiply words, since that effort will always fall short of total description, Montesquieu prefers to engage Melite's (and any other reader's) imagination and elicit her contribution to his description. This kind of cooperative text, constantly awaiting the active reader, is precisely what is required to make those erotic passages effective.

I have treated only some of Montesquieu's minor works, and each one only briefly. Yet, as this rapid review indicates, Montesquieu, even in his admittedly secondary writings, is sharpening the same analytic tools and reworking the same material as in his most mature works.

Chapter Seven
Mes Pensées

In addition to the volumes of excerpts, citations, and research notes discussed in chapter 6, Montesquieu also kept a working journal from about 1720 until his death. These three quarto volumes were published in 1899–1901 under the title *Pensées et fragments inédits de Montesquieu* (Montesquieu's unpublished thoughts and fragments). Today they are known simply as *Mes Pensées* (My thoughts). Interestingly, Barckhausen's edition of 1899–1901 did not respect the original order of Montesquieu's entries but renumbered them. In addition, the editor organized Montesquieu's text around his own topic headings. Despite such modifications, this has become the standard text for the *Pensées*. Barckhausen's numbering system and reordering of the original have been used by almost all modern editors.[1] While they are not Montesquieu's, Barckhausen's topic headings do indicate succinctly the scope and contents of the work:

Autobiographical Comments (with such subheadings as "His Character," "His Life," "His Family")
Comments on His Published Works
Fragments of projected works
Science and Industry ("Hygiene and Medicine," "Discoveries and Inventions," "Geography")
Arts and Letters
Psychology (with such subtitles as "Patriotism and Ambition," "Wit," "Virtues and Vices," "Women," "Ethnic Characteristics")
History
Political Education and Political Economics
Philosophy
Religion

These were subjects Montesquieu pondered throughout his life and in all his published works. They retained his attention even in these pages not intended for any reader other than himself.

Mes Pensées is a very curious book. It surely contains Montesquieu's words even though they are not presented exactly as he wrote them. Barckhausen's rearrangement by topic hides the order of composition and thus any potential clues to the development of Montesquieu's thinking through the years. By organizing the contents more logically, the editor has lost the spontaneity of the author recording his thoughts as they came to him and not bothering to arrange them. Obviously such a working notebook can not be read like a finished volume. By its very nature, it is always "in progress." Montesquieu stored, as it were, in these pages thoughts and ideas while he was developing them. This was his workshop where he labored over his material. Many of the projects, sketches, and drafts that fill these pages were eventually abandoned or considered not quite appropriate for publication. These notebooks thus provide a peek behind the scenes, a private viewing of a master crafts-man at work. Not everything in these pages is up to the standard we expect of Montesquieu. But it is precisely there that its value lies.

Mes Pensées is therefore more a potential than a realized book. What I find most fascinating about it is precisely that it is partial and incom-plete. The book does not conceal its unfinished aspect. Almost every-thing about it is raw and unready. In contrast to *The Persian Letters,* the author has no mask, anonymity, or narrator to hide behind. Here Mon-tesquieu speaks in his own voice. In contrast to the *Considerations* or *The Spirit of the Laws,* he has not fully refined his ideas so the reader is warned that what is said here may not be definitive. In these pages Montesquieu is at work, reviewing material he has thought about for years and still attempting to finalize his grasp on it. Occasionally we find passages that he will transfer whole to some other work. Mostly, however, the text contains the germ of ideas that have not yet reached fruition. This is a book of possibilities, of alternatives, of might-have-beens. In an author so typically eighteenth-century in his formality and in the careful reserve of his public style, these pages reveal Montesquieu in his shirt sleeves, the président at work in his library tower at La Brède.

My analysis will focus on this element of process, on the unfinished and fragmented nature of *Mes Pensées,* since the content is so similar to what we have already seen in the published works. By emphasizing this "unedited" element, I intend to offer an alternative to the traditional organization by content. My discussion will be divided into two sec-tions, each of which tries to capture one of Montesquieu's "attitudes" toward his text.

Copies, Echoes, and Fragments

The first attitude is structural or organizational. It emphasizes the tentative and unfinished nature of the text, and how these discontinuous remarks remain in an almost liquid state, ready to take on various shapes and forms. I am referring to pages that, having been developed here, became part of other works. Montesquieu himself indicates with his own footnotes certain passages that he incorporated into his published works. Such borrowing constitutes a primary function of these notebooks. Part laboratory and part workshop, these pages act like an intellectual storage shed. Various ideas, piled about in confusing jumbles, await their appropriate context.

However, material was not just copied out verbatim. Differences appear in the transfer, some major, some minor. The notebooks contain reformulations, echoes, repetitions of familiar material, versions that would eventually lead to more definitive formulations, but necessarily versions that were themselves not selected for publication. Among the most evident examples, the rise and fall of nations follows its own immutable path because "it is impossible that a nation founded on industry not falter from time to time, because the very prosperity it has enjoyed is dangerous and produces that decline" (*MP* 1773: 1425).[2] Montesquieu notes that this passage was used in his "Réflexions sur la monarchie universelle en Europe." However, the wording has changed slightly. Therefore this single citation illustrates two points. While it is a copy, transferred to another work, it is also an alternative, a variation that has not yet found its definitive form. To offer another example, one particularly felicitous phrase, which closely resembles a passage in the *Laws* (19:4) discussed above, sums up an essential point running throughout Montesquieu's thinking about causation: "Men are ruled by five different factors: climate, customs, mores, religion, and laws. Consequently, in every nation, when one of these causes acts with greater force, the others diminish proportionately" (*MP* 1903: 1458). While avoiding the simplistic automatism of which his historical determinism is often accused, this sentence neatly expresses the systemic interaction of those forces that Montesquieu studied in the *Laws* and the *Considerations*. It also reminds us that there are five equal, interacting factors, even though critics tend to focus on climate alone when discussing Montesquieu. As Jean Starobinski points out, Montesquieu's determinism is neither linear nor unicausal.[3] On the contrary, it derives from multiple causes, each of which competes with and yet complements the others in producing the final impulse that decides an event.

Number 615 is a long, detailed entry that argues in favor of the existence of God and against the materialism of Spinoza and the jungle of Hobbes. The title of the entry is "Continuation of some thoughts that did not go into the *Treatise on Duty*" (*MP* 615:1137), an obvious proof of the close connection between what Montesquieu expresses in these notebooks and the positions he argues in his other writings. Instead of losing this valuable idea completely, he stores it here. Instead of being obliged to publish or to cut the material, he retains it as variation and echo. The thought is not lost so much as displaced, temporarily disconnected but still full of potential, awaiting an appropriate context. In a sense, reading *Mes Pensées* undoes that disconnection and establishes a new connection. Lodged in the back of our mind, that fragment provides important additional material for any discussion of Montesquieu's thinking on atheism and religion by filling in some of the blanks left in the published material.

Closely related in spirit to these variations are the contradictions that appear in these numerous repetitions and reworkings of a limited amount of material. Since these notebooks were kept over a long period of time, they reflect and record the changing thought of the author through his life. To complicate matters, Montesquieu probably saw no need to eliminate what he had previously written when he changed his mind or advanced to another stage in his thinking. The purpose of the notebooks was, after all, to record for himself what he had thought at any one particular time. It is not surprising, then, that the final text— and we must remember that there is no "final" text here because this is essentially a work continuously in progress—contains entries that are not in complete agreement. What is surprising is that there are so few.

Nonetheless, at least one of these contradictions is worth mentioning. Number 1525 reads "all these great movements only happened because of some unplanned, unforeseen action. Lucrecia's death caused Tarquin's fall. Brutus's act of executing his sons established liberty. Seeing Virginia slain by her father caused the fall of the Ten" (*MP* 1525: 1368). In this fragment Montesquieu is arguing that spectacular events can mobilize public opinion in a manner and with a force that is totally unpredictable. Indeed, he used the same examples of Tarquin and Virginia when he examined the separation of powers as a brake on tyranny in the *Laws* (11:12 and 15). From the public's unsuspected and therefore unpredictable reaction flows a new social order. However,

Montesquieu seems to hold contradicting views on this point. In the *Considerations* (chapter 18), he stated that particular causes are really only symptoms of general causes. The latter are the deep causal motives. They can be expressed through any one of several more superficial factors. A similar viewpoint can be found in the notebooks where Montesquieu distinguishes between the general causes of the Protestant Reformation and Martin Luther, whom he considers only an accidental cause: "Martin Luther is credited with the Reformation. But it had to happen. If it had not been Luther, it would have been someone else. The arts and sciences coming from Greece had already opened eyes to abuses. Such a cause had to produce some effect. A proof of this: the councils of Constance and Basel had introduced a kind of reformation" (*MP* 2180:1566). Are there passages in the notebooks that contradict each other? Yes. Can these two "contradictory" thoughts on causation be easily reconciled? Perhaps, perhaps not. But what results from this confrontation is the awareness that Montesquieu's final thoughts were not the self-evident givens that his style so often makes it appear. Seeing him argue the evidence both for and against reveals an open-minded and inquisitive intelligence working out his ideological positions. If the principle of deep causation is, in fact, as innovative as critics claim, it is not at all surprising that Montesquieu did not discover it effortlessly. In these "thoughts" Montesquieu is actually thinking, struggling to find and define an historical law that will make sense of confusing human conduct.

In this same section I would also group some remarks that bring badly needed nuances to critical concepts. Too often do Montesquieu's ideas appear rigid and brittle. Part of this is stylistic. Montesquieu's elegant sentences, carefully constructed and counterbalanced, can give even to a tentative proposition the air of an irrefutable axiom. Thus, what some have seen as the absolute hegemony of climate over political institutions is really given nuance by the fact that immigrations and invasions also bring wholesale change in their wake: "From time to time there take place in the world those inundations of peoples that impose everywhere their customs and mores. The inundation of the Muslims brought despotism; the Northmen, the government of nobles. It took nine hundred years to abolish that government and to establish, in every state, monarchy. . . . That is why there has always been an ebb and flow of empire and liberty" (*MP* 1475:1353–4). When Montesquieu tries to balance the coexistence of king and freedom, is he contradicting himself or making a subtle point that complicates oversimplified notions about the nature of monarchy and republic? "I used to say: 'If there were no king in England, the English would be less free.' That can be proven by Holland where the people have been in greater slavery ever since the stadholder has ceased to exist: all the magistrates in every town are tyrants" (*MP* 1674:1402). The Dutch Republic was usually regarded in the eighteenth century as the show-place of liberty and as the concrete proof that self-rule could work. Laws are not immutable nor are they automatic in their effects. The same laws produce different results in different circumstances because "laws make good and bad citizens. The same timid spirit that will make a man faithful to his duties in a republic will make a shifty man in another. The same audacious spirit that will cause a man to love his country and to sacrifice himself for it in one state, will make him a highway robber in another" (*MP* 1755:1419). Montesquieu's final po-sition, as noted above, is that history and society are the complex result of a web of five principal strands. Interweaving and interconnected, acting and reacting, each single strand changes as the others do.

Let us also note that inside the notebooks there are multiple vari-ations on a single theme. When Montesquieu records several versions of one idea, he is working on phrasing and syntax, polishing his prose until he gets it just right. Numbers 1104 and 1105 are practically identical, distinguished from each other by only a few words, while 1331 and 1332 differ more substantially even as they make the same point.

I am afraid of the Jesuits. If I offend a nobleman, he will forget me, I will forget him, I will move to another province, another country. But, if I offend the Jesuits in Rome, I will find them in Paris; everywhere they will surround me. Their habit of writing to each other extends their antipathies. An enemy of the Jesuits is like an enemy of the Inquisition: he finds their intimate friends everywhere. (*MP* 1331:1320)

The Jesuits, I fear them. They're a body that envelopes me, that can find me anywhere. Let me offend a nobleman, I will go away and I will never see him again. But the Jesuits are like the intimate friends of the Inquisition (*MP* 1332:1320–1).

The second text is pithier and more direct, while the first explores the consequences and ramifications of the situation in more convincing detail. Montesquieu noted the connection between these two entries, which were not sequential in his manuscript. It was Barckhausen's 1899 edition that first put these thoughts back to back. If we lose thereby the chance to find such connections ourselves, we better appreciate the impact of their juxtaposition. This single confrontation of two similar texts illustrates how *Mes Pensées* is not a definitive text but rather one in progress. No choice, selection, or elimination of various "thoughts" has to be made. Variations, alternatives, and competing versions can all remain. Nothing has to be cut. Themes are allowed to echo inside these pages, ideas can bear both repetition and modification.

A final subset of entries picks up on the device of fragmentation. There are passages that appear to be broken off from other works, separated from their original context or their ultimate destination. Occasionally we find what looks like a letter. Number 1656 begins with the date "2 February 1742," and ends with a traditional epistolary closing, "Adieu, Monsieur, I speak to you as a good Frenchman. . . ." Is this a real letter or just a fictional exercise on a political theme? In the section on French politics, there is an entire letter (*MP* 1878:1446) addressed "To the Baron De Stein" and dated "Amsterdam, 20 October 1729." In the section on English politics, one entry is addressed like a letter "To Mr. Domville" and it begins: "You ask me, sir, what I think of the longevity of the English government and to predict what will be the consequences of its corruption" (*MP* 1883:1447). Before the letter ends, however, it adopts the tone and has stretched to the length of an essay. Similarly, there are whole sections entitled (by Barckhausen, of course) "Letters" and "Discourses" that are nothing but fragments of those two genres. Sometimes the entry is long and well developed, other times it is just a line or two. Some of these letters seem to be legitimate: "You wrote me, dear father, that you will not mention to my uncles the reasons you have to complain of me" (*MP* 506:1039). Doubtless this is an echo, perhaps even a preliminary draft or copy, of a letter dating back to Montesquieu's student days in Paris before he assumed the title and office of his uncle Jean-Baptiste. But is the following a real letter, a trace of those rambunctious years in the free and easy Paris of the Regency, or it is a sketch for an oriental and erotic fiction? "You are leaving me then, and you are leaving me for a man of no merit. How unhappy I am! What greater misfortune could befall me than to see myself obliged to blush for having loved you. . . ." (*MP* 510:1040). In the same amorous vein, the following excerpt is a bit more moving in its greater detail and its use of the familiar *tu* (you): "I am disconsolate. Imagine that I am still in that horrible state we both were when we parted. Do you remember that, my dearest? Did your own distress allow you to notice the full extent of mine?" (*MP* 512:1042). Such passages present a real conundrum. Are they traces of the various love affairs imputed to Montesquieu while in Paris? Or are they mere literary exercises, trial passages and unused material originally intended for titillating novels like the *Temple de Gnide*?

A number of entries begin "I said . . ." We remember this formula from the travel notebooks where Montesquieu recorded various conversations he participated in. Here the formula often appears to conclude a dialogue or an argument. Is Montesquieu setting down his conclusion, his "punch line," expecting to add the lead-in later? "I said to Monsieur the Duke that he was always looking for the truth and always missing it" (*MP* 1638:1395). Number 2182 provides two short paragraphs of dialogue on the need for patience in adversity. In a footnote Montesquieu explains that he "was having a Quaker speak to the king of England" (*MP* 2182:1567). We do not know any more about its context or the author's intentions. Nonetheless, this cryptic note suggests perhaps an imitation of Voltaire's *Philosophical Letters* or at least some work combining fictional devices and philosophic content.

Self-Reflections and Personal Values

The second "attitude" permeating this text would be Montesquieu's more intimate and personal feelings, his private judgments both on his method of work and on the material itself. To begin, I point to those self-reflective remarks that touch upon methodology. Montesquieu is not a naive writer. He is a conscious craftsman and an intelligent historian who goes about his work aware of what he wants to accomplish and how he can best do it. In the privacy of his notebooks he reveals more about his working habits than elsewhere. "In order to write well, you have to jump over intermediary ideas just enough so as not to be boring, not too much for fear of not being understood" (*MP* 802:1220). This entry goes a long way in explaining the organization of *The Spirit of the Laws* which is often said to be an accumulation of examples without the necessary transitions and connections. Montesquieu prefers juxtaposition to transition, parataxis to syntaxis, or, in movie jargon, the jump cut to the smooth segue. His tendency to wander off the main topic and into the imposing mass of scholarly details is not a fault but a virtue in his own eyes because "those who make digressions think they are like men with long arms and who can therefore reach further" (*MP* 812:1223). While a regular and controlled writer himself in the tradition of the seventeenth century, Montesquieu understands that French classicism always runs the danger of allowing its fascination with symmetry to degenerate into monotony. "Too much regularity is sometimes and even often disagreeable. Nothing is as beautiful as the sky; but it is strewn randomly with stars. The mansions and gardens around Paris have the fault of being too much the same. They are continual copies of Le Nôtre" (*MP* 985:1265). The président already hears the changes coming, the new style and inspiration that romanticism will bring to society, to literature, and even to gardens.

Perhaps the most significant methodological statement is found in the following passage where Montesquieu acknowledges his own bias as an historian. He identifies the dilemma that opposes the need to know numerous details and to sink deeply into the pieces of history against the need for a coherent interpretation of the whole: "You do not invent a system after having read history; but you begin with the system and then you seek the proof. There are so many facts in a long history, people have thought so differently, the beginnings are usually so obscure that you always find enough to support all kinds of reactions" (*MP* 1582:1382–3). This advice will not work for everyone and many would disagree. Still, it does indicate the priority of theory in Montesquieu's own work. He used his extensive readings to provide the concrete details that would illustrate the secret functioning of historical and social "laws" that his theory alone could explain.

A quite different entry is worth mentioning even if it does not admit an easy interpretation. Having labored over the barren fields of law and jurisprudence, Montesquieu surely appreciated the need for some relaxation from that dry scholarship. But is he entirely serious when he complains that "to please in a vain and frivolous conversation is today the only merit. For that, the magistrate abandons the study of law. . . . We flee, as if it were pernicious, any study that might eliminate playfulness" (*MP* 1193:1300). This is perhaps an overstatement, an extreme position that Montesquieu entertains for a moment before dismissing it. He did, after all, devote 20 years of hard study and writing to his *The Spirit of the Laws*. Such a paradoxical thought only serves to underline the unfinished nature of *Mes Pensées* and how difficult it is to draw hard and fast conclusions from so elusive a text. Seen from another angle, this brief fragment might be nothing more than a variation on the classical dictum of joining the useful and the pleasurable.

Montesquieu himself joined high seriousness with frivolity in *The Persian Letters* and never did allow his studies to keep him long from the social life of the capital.

Last, but certainly not least, are a number of remarks that emphasize Montesquieu's personal and human values. Here he can forget his role as scholar and indulge his own emotional reaction to what he has studied. Listen, for example, to his moral outrage when he discusses the Spanish treatment of Indians in South America: "We cannot reflect without indignation upon the cruelties that the Spanish inflicted on the Indians and, when we are forced to write on this subject, we cannot stop ourselves from using the high theatrical tone" (*MP* 1573:1370). Readers have not found in the *Laws,* for example, a simple condemnation of abuses like slavery. They are often uneasy with Montesquieu's ironic handling of that issue. In these more personal and intimate pages, he can express the deep feelings that he might not have wanted to include in a work of objective scholarship.

Still, Montesquieu was not afraid to stake out his moral position loud and clear when he felt compelled to do so. Some of his remarks were clearly dangerous for the times in which he lived. In an abandoned project for a history of France, he criticizes the powerful minister of war under Louis XIV, "Louvois, the worst Frenchman who perhaps was ever born" (*MP* 595:1121). He indicts "the two worst citizens that France ever had: Richelieu and Louvois" (*MP* 595:1120). Further on he notes that "Cardinal Dubois was a real cad" (*MP* 596:1124). He does not hesitate to express a very low opinion of Louis XIV in a detailed pen-portrait: "He had more the mediocre qualities of a king than the great ones . . . born with a mediocre mind. He often mistook false grandeur for the real. . . . Very easy to deceive. . . . Toward the end of his life, difficult to amuse; incapable of seeking or of finding resources within himself; no reading, no passion; saddened by religious devotion, and with his old wife, delivered up to the grief of an old king" (*MP* 596:1123–4). By no means is this a complimentary evaluation, either of the Sun King or his spouse, Mme de Maintenon. Criticizing Louis later for revoking the Edict of Nantes and thus destroying the economic vitality of the country, Montesquieu says he "pities him more than the Huguenots" (*MP* 1617:1390) whom he forced into exile.

As a close observer of French life and a student of her history, Montesquieu comes close to being a prophet on a few occasions. One entry pinpoints the opportunities of meritocracy within the chaos of civil strife. What Montesquieu describes or imagines here was later realized by the Revolution of 1789: "There is no state as dangerous and as liable to menace others with conquest, as a state in the throes of civil war. It is because all the people (nobles, bourgeois, workers) become soldiers. Besides, great men are formed then because, in the confusion, those who have merit break through while, in contrast, men are chosen when the state is tranquil, and they are chosen badly" (*MP* 1481:1356). Not only does this passage suggest why the untested volunteers in the revolutionary army of 1793 beat the best-trained armies of Europe, but also why a Bonaparte emerged from the chaos of the French Revolution and the Reign of Terror. The same passage is not without insight into the American Revolution, which pitted colonist-farmers against British regulars and produced our Founding Fathers. Montesquieu seems to foresee a situation that will become a famous military action and political maneuver: "A king of France or Spain, with 30,000 men and a well-equipped fleet, would conquer all of Egypt. . . . Egypt always conquered in one swoop. Still a country easy to protect, except from the sea" (*MP* 1498:1361). Napoleon's military conquest was undone by Nelson's naval victory at Aboukir.

In conclusion, *Mes Pensées* is a compilation of fragments articulated around the same corpus of material that Montesquieu worked and reworked in his published books. The lightness of touch that can be found here and that is missing in, for example, *The Spirit of the Laws*, is counterbalanced by a fragmentation and a digressiveness that prevent any sustained point of view or consideration of a single topic. First and foremost this is a text without clearly fixed and stable meanings, a shifting text that avoids neat conclusions. A composite of bits and pieces, it does not coalesce into a coherent whole no matter how tantalizing and provocative its individual parts may be. In the end it exemplifies the zigzag approach that avoids intermediary steps and the necessary chain of logical reasoning. *Mes Pensées* lacks the central alleyway and the single, dominating perspective that was the defining element of the French garden. More like the English landscape garden, with its sinuous paths and its incongruous combinations of heterogeneous plants and materials, Montesquieu's "thoughts" amble along more attentive to the detail at hand than the overall design. Like the English garden, this text promises a surprise around the next bend and allows its readers to wander as they will through its rich diversity.

Chapter Eight

Conclusions

When he died in 1755 Montesquieu enjoyed an international reputation as one of the most important writers of his century. That near universal acclaim was based on *The Spirit of the Laws* and the impact it had on political thinking throughout Europe and indeed the entire Western world. Montesquieu cast a shadow over political thought that endured for almost two centuries. He did lose favor during the most extreme phases of the French Revolution, especially the Reign of Terror. Given Montesquieu's ideological positions, this is in no way surprising or unexpected, however. Throughout the nineteenth and into the twentieth century, he remained the standard reference for political discussion even as his work inspired new initiatives in the social sciences. Durkheim called Montesquieu the "father of sociology," thereby indicating his debt as well as passing on to Montesquieu the paternal role often accorded to him. Other disciplines such as political science, political economics, cultural anthropology, and ethnology evolved from Montesquieu's pioneering efforts. But eventually the président fell victim to his own success. Redundant and considered out-of-date in the very social sciences he helped so much to found, Montesquieu's masterpiece was read only in snippets and by an ever decreasing audience. While never eliminated from the university curriculum, he was nonetheless allowed to gather dust in the corner, alluded to but not really read, an ancestor whose name was remembered but whose active presence was no longer required. It was only in the 1960s, after ground-breaking work by Roger Laufer and Jean Starobinski, that Montesquieu was again perceived as a vital writer, one whose work had not been exhausted by time and familiarity and who now demanded renewed attention and rereading. In the 30 years since that critical watershed, Montesquieu has been restored to a place of honor. But that place has changed considerably. No longer does Montesquieu dominate the social sciences. Now he is almost exclusively a literary figure, relegated to French departments and to professors of literature. Like Voltaire and Diderot, he is one of those curious hybrids typical of the eighteenth century who belong to the world of letters precisely because they were interested in so many things besides letters.

Perhaps the most important conclusion I would draw from this study is the realization that Montesquieu is a diverse and elusive author. No longer is he the man of one book. In addition to the *Laws*, he must be read and understood through *The Persian Letters* and the *Considerations*, as a traveler on the grand tour, and as a scholar at home with his books and his "Thoughts." He is the jurist from a family of magistrates, a large landowner running a successful wine-growing business. He is a writer concerned with the most critical political issues of his time as well as the author of frothy oriental tales, tinged with his personal blend of wit and eroticism. He is both the provincial gentleman living in the countryside at La Brède and the Parisian sophisticate, visiting the capital for extended periods of time and frequenting the fashionable salons there. He is a complex man whose final word is often ambiguous, who leaves contradictions unresolved in his texts, who often weighs the pros and cons to the point of frustrating equilibrium. The old picture of Montesquieu depicted him as the archetypical Enlightenment thinker clearly limned in full light and without shadows. That picture has to be changed into a much more modern and perplexing portrait that captures his playful irony, his love of indirection and innuendo, his ability to elude easy categorization.

A second conclusion would be to underline the new center of gravity that has developed in the last 30 years of Montesquieu studies. While a good deal of the "literary" criticism now devoted to Montesquieu remains traditional in that it continues to focus on ideas, on philosophy and politics, on moral and social issues, a newer trend is coming to the fore. This reevaluation is more properly literary in that it balances questions of form and expression with those of content: witness the attention being given to *The Persian Letters* as a fiction and a novel rather than as a sociological document or an early draft of the *Laws*. In terms of current critical interest and scholarship (as my bibliography demonstrates quite convincingly), *The Persian Letters* is arguably as important a work as the *Laws*. There is no doubt that it has more readers and has generated more excitement and controversy with the recent reinterpretations based on the "secret chain" and the function of the harem intrigue. If that novel is not yet at the center of Montesquieu's work, it is fast becoming an equal partner.

As a consequence of the newfound status and weight of *The Persian Letters* in Montesquieu's total output, my study has been oriented in the direction of narrative. Showing how Montesquieu's interest in politics and social life can be fictionalized effectively reconciles what some see as an antagonism between *The Persian Letters* as a novel and as a sociological essay. The chapter on the *Voyages* attempts to read those notebooks as an early travel narrative or the story of Montesquieu's grand tour as told by himself. The short fiction in his minor works has been emphasized, both for their ideological content and their fictional form. The two complement each other, here as elsewhere. Finally, I have chosen to discuss as narrative a number of the tales, anecdotes, or parables that are interspersed throughout the *Laws*. Short and to the point, both allusive and elusive, often filled with the personal commitment that Montesquieu withholds elsewhere, these are effective stories in the best tradition of the eighteenth-century *conte*.

Overall my interpretations have consisted in revisiting traditional positions and updating them. I have considered the intellectual stimulation of *The Persian Letters* as depending in large part on the ambiguities and contradictions created by its fictional presentation. I have discussed the *Considerations* as a key example of eighteenth-century historiography, both for its relation to other historians of that time and for its own unique way of "doing" history. I have devoted what might seem overly long discussions to the minor works, including the *Voyages* and the *Pensées*. These are badly in need of serious consideration, however, and this refocusing of attention is, it seems to me, entirely warranted. Finally, I have emphasized the modernity of Montesquieu's thinking whenever appropriate. His discussion of money and its symbolic metavalue in the *Laws* stands out as one such detail that strikes a very contemporary note.

Continuing with this last issue of modernity, my study demonstrates how relevant Montesquieu is to today's political and social reality. The terms that Montesquieu employs in his analysis of government (e.g., virtue, honor, duty, education, formation, frugality) are terms that are sorely lacking in today's political discourse. But they are just as sorely needed. Montesquieu explains in human terms how government works, how good government depends on good citizenship, and how citizens must behave to obtain the kind of government they want. It would be foolish to claim that Montesquieu has ready answers to any of today's baffling questions. However, he does give us the means of asking those questions correctly, and he indicates where and how to look for the best responses. His thoughts on the corrupting effects of slavery and the second-class citizenship of women are as pertinent now as they were 200 years ago, if not more so. He reminds us continually to take the global view and to see everything in the widest context possible. He repeats constantly that events are the products of multiple factors and that these factors are themselves multiple and interrelated. Behind observable phenomena he discovers complex interweavings of causations rather than any single, and therefore simple-minded, cause. Indeed, his conviction that real causes are deep and invisible and must not be mistaken for superficial symptoms is a methodological constant that bears reiteration for modern readers. In his extensive documentation Montesquieu illustrates how manners, mores, and customs influence laws. He shows how and where the edge of unconscious behavior meets the realm of rational thought. Whole pages could be excerpted from Montesquieu and added as footnotes to our newspapers, for they chronicle the same conflicts, the same problems that he identified and analyzed. Montesquieu is full of details that seem to have been written only yesterday.

As our American Constitution enters its third century, it remains an incredible illustration of practical political thinking married to theoretical speculation. It has animated the most long-lived, unbroken, and continuous government in modern times. While constitutions in other countries, even in an old democracy like France, have come and gone during that same period, ours has endured. Even as we celebrate the Constitution's remarkable ability to adjust to changing conditions, theorists debate its exact meaning. Strict construction or loose, the Framers' original intentions, the right to interpolate from contemporary documents—all these issues can benefit from reading and understanding Montesquieu. As the chief political theorist of his time, Montesquieu wielded an enormous influence over those who drafted our Constitution.[1] The source and conduit for much of what was known about the ancient worlds of Greece and Rome, he was the acknowledged authority on republican government throughout the eighteenth century. Thomas Jefferson and Benjamin Franklin had perhaps the closest contact with Montesquieu due to their sojourns in France. But all the Founding Fathers and the Framers of the Constitution were aware of his ideas and took his opinions into consideration. Montesquieu is closer to home and to today's current events than we might at first think.

In the end I hope that revisiting Montesquieu has captured the excitement of his work and communicated it in turn. Under the accumulated dust of misconception and forgetfulness, Montesquieu is a modern writer, wrestling with problems of narrative that are quite contemporary, voicing a vision of society that accentuates the importance of the human factor, and reminding us of the complex forces that influence human behavior. Between the inarticulate, instinctual pull of culture and ethnicity on the one hand and the rational voice of law and conscious decision making on the other, Montesquieu locates a universe peopled with fictions like Usbek and crammed with the facts documented in the *Considerations* and the *Laws*. That universe, so eighteenth-century in Montesquieu's pages, is also our own. Revisiting him is to find ourselves. The trip is well worth taking.

Notes and References

Chapter One

1. See Jonathan D. Spence, *The Question of Hu* (New York: Knopf, 1988), who tells the story of this Chinese traveler in France.
2. "Cela sera vendu comme du pain." Quoted in "Chronologie," Montesquieu, *Oeuvres complètes,* ed. Daniel Oster (Paris: Editions du Seuil, 1964), 11. The translation here as elsewhere throughout this book is my own.
3. "Eloge historique de M. de Montesquieu, par M. de Secondat, son fils" (Historical account of Montesquieu by his son), in Montesquieu, *Oeuvres complètes,* ed. Daniel Oster (Paris: Editions du Seuil, 1964), 16.
4. See Robert Shackleton, *Montesquieu: A Critical Biography* (Oxford: Oxford University Press, 1961), pp. 393f, where the deathbed scene is recounted in detail.

Chapter Two

1. Montesquieu, "Quelques Réflexions sur les *Lettres persanes,*" in *Oeuvres complètes,* Collection L'Intégrale, ed. Daniel Oster (Paris: Seuil, 1964), 62.
2. Montesquieu, *Les Lettres persanes,* in *Oeuvres complètes,* Collection L'Intégrale, ed. Daniel Oster (Paris: Seuil, 1964), Letter 30. Hereafter cited in text as *PL.* Citations will indicate the letter number rather than the page because that method will facilitate reference to any edition. All translations are my own.
3. The edition of 1758, although published posthumously, contained 161 letters and reflected Montesquieu's last corrections and revisions. The earlier editions of 1721 and 1754 had fewer letters. The text published most frequently today is that of 1758.
4. Jean-Jacques Rousseau, "Discourse on the Arts and Sciences" (1750) and "Discourse on the Origins of Inequality" (1755). Both essays were entered in competitions sponsored by the Académie of Dijon. The Académie's question in 1749 was "whether the reestablishment of arts and sciences has contributed to purifying mores" and Rousseau's answer, published the following year, won. The simple fact of opening a national competition on this issue and the fame Rousseau acquired by his response indicate how burning a "question" (literally since the topics were phrased as questions) this was. Cosmopolitan and sophisticated in marked contrast to the boorish and unsociable Rousseau, Voltaire incarnated the brilliant society he defended with wit and grace in all his writings, but especially in his light verse.

5. See the bibliography for the most important of the numerous articles that examine "the secret chain."

6. See Robert Shackleton, "Montesquieu's Moslem Chronology," *French Studies* 8 (1954): 17–27. See also Melvin Richter, *The Political Theory of Montesquieu* (Cambridge: Cambridge University Press, 1977), 141–42.

7. Few critics have analyzed the time problem at the end of *The Persian Letters*. Some interesting interpretations of this tricky issue can be found, however, in Pierre Testud, "Les *Lettres persanes*, roman épistolaire," *Revue d'Histoire Littéraire* 66 (1966): 642–656; Jean Goldzink, *Les Lettres persanes*, Études Littéraires (Paris: Presses Universitaires de France, 1989); and Nick Roddick, "The Structure of the *Lettres persanes*," *French Studies* 28 (1974): 397–407.

Chapter Three

1. See Micheline F. Harris, "Le Séjour de Montesquieu en Italie (août 1728–juillet 1729): Chronologie et commentaires," *Studies on Voltaire and the Eighteenth Century* 127 (1974): 65–197. Italy bulks largest in the text of his travels.

2. Montesquieu, *Voyages en Europe* in *Oeuvres complètes*, Collection L'Intégrale, ed. Daniel Oster (Paris: Seuil, 1964), 213d. All citations will be to this edition and will be indicated parenthetically as *VE* followed by a page number. The text is printed in double columns in small characters, so there is a good deal of material on each page. I will add the letters *a* through *d* to refer to the four quarters of each page. Thus *a* indicates the upper left (top of first column), *b* the lower left (bottom of first column), *c* the upper right (top of second column) and *d* the lower right (bottom of second column). All translations are my own.

3. Georges Van Den Abbeele, "Montesquieu *touriste*, or a View from the Top," *L'Esprit Créateur* 25, no. 3 (Fall 1985): 64–74.

4. On the whole topic of art and Montesquieu, see Jean Ehrard, *Montesquieu, critique d'art* (Paris: Presses Universitaires de France, 1965).

Chapter Four

1. Jacques-Bénigne Bossuet, *Discours sur l'histoire universelle* (Paris: Garnier-Flammarion, 1966), 427; hereafter cited as *Discourse*. My translation.

2. Patrick Henry, "Contre Barthes," *Studies on Voltaire and the Eighteenth Century* 249 (1987), 24.

3. Montesquieu, *"Lettres persanes" and "Considérations"* (Paris: Classiques Larousse, 1952), 72. My translation.

4. Montesquieu, *Considérations sur les causes de la grandeur des Romains et de leur décadence*, in *Oeuvres complètes*, Collection l'Intégrale, ed. David Oster (Paris: Seuil, 1964), 445a. All citations will be to this edition. Hereafter cited in text as *Considerations*. Translations are my own.

5. Metaphor is not usually studied in Montesquieu. See, however, Jane McLelland, "Metaphor in Montesquieu's Theoretical Writings," *Studies on Voltaire and the Eighteenth Century* 199 (1981): 205–24, and Georges Benrekassa, "Système métaphorique et pensée politique: Montesquieu et l'imagination mécanique dans *L'Esprit des lois*," *Revue des Sciences Humaines* 3 (1982): 241–255.

Chapter Five

1. André Lagarde et Laurent Michard, *Le XVIIIième Siècle* (Paris: Bordas, 1969), 94–95.

2. Jean Lecomte, *Montesquieu,* Collection Littérature "Expliquez-moi . . ." (Paris: Les Editions Foucher, 1964), 30–36.

3. Montesquieu, *De l'Esprit des Lois,* in *Oeuvres complètes,* vol 2, ed. Roger Caillois (Paris: Pléiade, 1951). All quotations will be from this edition, upon which I have based my translations. To enable the reader to use any edition whether in French or in translation, however, I will use the following system of references. The first number refers to the book, the second to the chapter. The third number gives the page or pages in the Pléiade edition. Thus (12:3:432) should be read: book 12, chapter 3, page 432 in the Pléiade. If there are only two numbers, they refer to the book and the entire chapter. Material that precedes the first book will be indicated as "Avertissement de l'auteur" (Author's note) with the Pléiade page number only.

4. Charles Kunstler, *La Vie Quotidienne sous Louis XV* (Paris: Hachette, 1953), 240–42.

5. On this, see the old but still valuable Paul Spurlin, *Montesquieu en Amérique* (University, La.: Louisiana State University Press, 1940). Also his "Montesquieu et la constitution américaine," *Actes du Congrès Montesquieu* (Bordeaux: Imprimerie Delmas, 1956). More recently, see Paul Vernière, "Montesquieu et la constitution américaine," in *Travaux de Littérature* (Paris: ADIREL, 1989), 2:209–17.

6. The place of England in Montesquieu's thinking is an enormous topic. See, for example, Lando Landi, *L'Inghilterra e il pensiero politico di Montesquieu* (Padua, Italy: CEDAM, 1981).

7. See Robert O'Reilly, "Montesquieu: Anti-feminist," *Studies on Voltaire and the Eighteenth Century* 102 (1973), 143–56. Also see Paul Hoffmann, "Un Montesquieu antiféministe," *Travaux de Linguistique et de Littérature* (Strasbourg) 18, no. 2 (1980): 133–43. For a more general treatment, see Jeannette Geffriaud-Rosso, *Montesquieu et la Féminité* (Paris: Nizet, 1978).

8. See James Fallows, "Wake Up, America!," *New York Review of Books,* 1 March 1990, 14–23. He opens with a paragraph that shows how contemporary Montesquieu's approach is: "Economists don't like to talk about the effects of culture or of ethics on economic development, since these are such subjective and imprecise matters. But most people, including economists off-duty, as-

sume that there is a connection between the kinds of everyday behavior a society encourages and its stability and prosperity" (p. 14).

9. See Simon Schama, *Citizens: A Chronicle of the French Revolution* (New York: Alfred Knopf, 1989), especially pp. 112–21. This theme runs throughout the book.

10. This essay is discussed in, chapter 6, Minor Works.

11. In the Pléiade edition, the sixth part runs to 216 pages or 28.6 percent of the 765 pages given over to the *Laws*.

12. Little has been done comparing these two writers. For Dubos, see Alfred Lombard, *L'Abbé Du Bos: Un Initiateur de la pensée moderne (1670–1742)* (Paris: Hachette, 1913). For Boulainvilliers, Harold A. Ellis, *Boulainvilliers and the French Monarchy: Aristocratic Politics in Early Eighteenth-Century France* (Ithaca, NY: Cornell University Press, 1988).

Chapter Six

1. Montesquieu, *Oeuvres complètes,* Collection L'Intégrale, ed. David Oster (Paris: Seuil, 1964), 159a. All citations will be to this text. Hereafter cited in text as *Oeuvres complètes*. All translations are my own.

2. The second paragraph of this essay begins: "We saw in book 14 of *The Spirit of the Laws* how heat and cold. . . ." It was written therefore after book 14, but we cannot say how long afterward.

3. Little has been written on these minor novels. See, however, Jean-Noel Pascal, "Montesquieu romancier après les *Lettres persanes*: Note sur *Arsace et Isménie,* histoire orientale," *Littératures* 17 (Autumn 1987): 85–91.

Chapter Seven

1. André Masson has published the *Pensées* in their original order. However, his edition is not easily available. It is not the standard reference for other editions and consequently not the version usually read.

2. Montesquieu, *Mes Pensées,* in *Oeuvres complètes,* vol 1, ed. Roger Caillois (Paris: Pléiade, 1951). References to this edition will be indicated parenthetically *MP* in the text. All translations are my own. To facilitate the use of other editions, I will give the Barckhausen number before the page, thus (*MP* 1779: 1425). The number is 1779 and it is on page 1425 in the Pléiade.

3. Jean Starobinski, *Montesquieu par lui-même,* Ecrivains de Toujours (Paris: Seuil, 1953), 81.

Chapter Eight

1. See Robert Wernick, "The Godfather of the American Constitution," *Smithsonian,* September 1989, pp. 183–96.

Selected Bibliography

This selected bibliography focuses on the last 30 years, in particular the scholarship that has emphasized the literary aspects of Montesquieu's work. The marked change in critical interest that took place during this period, for example, regarding the *Lettres persanes* as a novel, is highlighted here.

PRIMARY WORKS

In French

Montesquieu. *Oeuvres complètes*. 2 vols. Edited by Roger Caillois. Paris: Pléiade, 1949–51.
Montesquieu. *Oeuvres complètes*. Collection L'Intégrale. Edited by Daniel Oster. Paris: Seuil, 1964.
Montesquieu. *Oeuvres complètes*. 3 vols. Paris: Nagel, 1951–55. Edited by André Masson.

Translations

Montesquieu. *Selected Political Writings*. Rev. ed. Translated and edited by Melvin Richter. Indianapolis: Hackett, 1990.
Montesquieu. *The Persian Letters*. Translated by C. J. Betts. New York: Penguin, 1973.
Montesquieu. *The Spirit of the Laws*. Translated by Anne Cohler, Basia Miller, and Harold Stone. Cambridge: Cambridge University Press, 1989.
Montesquieu. *The Spirit of the Laws*. Translated by Thomas Nugent. New York: Hafner Press, 1949.
Montesquieu. *The Spirit of the Laws: A Compendium of the First English Edition with an English Translation of "An Essay on Causes Affecting Mind and Characters."* Translated by David Carrithers. Berkeley and Los Angeles: University of California Press, 1978.

SECONDARY SOURCES

Books

Althusser, Louis. *Montesquieu: La Politique et l'histoire.* 1959. Reprint. Paris: Presses Universitaires de France, 1965. A stimulating discussion and reevaluation that gives life to the traditional "marble image" of Montesquieu. Althusser discusses Montesquieu's historical method and his Newtonian approach to law.

Baum, John Alan. *Montesquieu and Social Theory.* Oxford, England: Pergamon, 1979. Argues that Montesquieu is a "founding father" of sociology who employed, even if only in embryonic form, critical concepts later developed by Emile Durkheim and Max Weber, especially the "ideal-type" analysis.

Benrekassa, Georges. *Montesquieu: La Liberté et l'histoire.* Paris: Garnier-Flammarion, 1987. A difficult, ambitious book that tries to demonstrate Montesquieu's specific modernity while analyzing the role of liberty in his concept of history. Benrekassa dialogues with contemporary critics of Montesquieu, especially Althusser.

―――. *Montesquieu.* Collection SUP Philosophes. Paris: Presses Universitaires de France, 1968. A short, concise discussion of Montesquieu as a political philosopher destined for the philosophy classes in lycées. Includes excerpts from Montesquieu's writings.

Cohler, Anne M. *Montesquieu's Comparative Politics and the Spirit of American Constitutionalism.* Lawrence: University Press of Kansas, 1988. Seeks the concealed coherence of *The Spirit of the Laws* in the concepts of spirit, moderation, and liberty in all their contexts. Has chapters on the American Constitution and on Tocqueville, and on how they compare to Montesquieu.

Desgraves, Louis. *Montesquieu.* Paris: Mazarine, 1986. An excellent biography that gives thorough treatment to the details of Montesquieu's life and his physical and cultural milieu.

Ehrard, Jean. *Montesquieu, critique d'art.* Paris: Presses Universitaires de France, 1965. A close analysis of Montesquieu's comments on Italian art (architecture, sculpture, painting) in his *Voyages.* Ehrard describes Montesquieu's initiation into the world of art and the values by which he made his aesthetic judgments.

Goldzink, Jean. *Montesquieu. Lettres persanes.* Etudes Littéraires. Paris: Presses Universitaires de France, 1989. This provocative reading highlights the ambiguities and the difficulties of reaching conclusions about such an indirect text. Perhaps too clever, it tries so hard to dazzle that at times it fails to illuminate.

Hulliung, Mark. *Montesquieu and the Old Regime.* Berkeley and Los Angeles: University of California Press, 1976. A reevaluation of Montesquieu's politics, seeing him as the most astute Machiavellian of the old regime and as a committed theorist of liberty and justice.

Laufer, Roger. *Style rococo, style des lumières.* Paris: José Corti, 1963. Reprints his seminal essay on the secret chain with a number of others.

Lecomte, J. *Montesquieu.* Paris: Foucher, 1964. A good French *manuel scolaire* intended for students preparing for the *bac* that provides outlines and analyses of the major works in a brief and easy-to-consult format.

Loy, J. Robert. *Montesquieu.* New York: Twayne, 1968. An excellent introduction to all Montesquieu's work with the bulk of attention going to *The Spirit of the Laws.*

Pangle, Thomas L. *Montesquieu's Philosophy of Liberalism: A Commentary on "The Spirit of the Laws."* Chicago: University of Chicago Press, 1973. A close reading of Montesquieu's major text. It brings out his principal ideas clearly and explains them in their historical context.

Quoniam, Théodore. *Introduction à une lecture de "L'Esprit des lois."* Archives des Lettres Modernes, no. 166. Paris: Minard, 1976. A short but solid overview with an emphasis on the legal aspects of the text. One chapter focuses on ideas still relevant and vital today.

Richter, Melvin. *The Political Theory of Montesquieu.* Cambridge: Cambridge University Press, 1977. Focuses on well-known elements like natural law, the typology of governments, and *esprit général.* Half of the text consists of translations from a variety of Montesquieu's works.

Shackleton, Robert. *Montesquieu.* Oxford: Oxford University Press, 1961. A classic biography and still the definitive work on Montesquieu's life.

Shklar, Judith. *Montesquieu.* Oxford: Oxford University Press, 1987. An excellent short survey of Montesquieu's principal works done from the perspective of an historian.

Starobinski, Jean. *Montesquieu par lui-même.* Ecrivains de toujours. Paris: Seuil, 1953. A provocative study filled with fine discussions and concepts like "transparent vision" and "negative liberty." One of the interpretations that reoriented scholarship on Montesquieu. Starobinski was among the first to recognize the *Lettres persanes* as a novel and to take the harem intrigue seriously.

Waddicor, Mark Hurlstone. *Montesquieu, Lettres persanes.* London: Arnold, 1977. A short but thorough analysis. He discusses the fiction but is more interested in the philosophical and social satire.

Articles

Benrekassa, Georges. "Le Parcours idéologique des *Lettres persanes*: Figures de la socialité et discours politique." *Europe* 574 (1977): 60–79. Despite its pretentious style, an interesting discussion of this novel in terms of the two literary genres, satire and political discourse, whose conventions it explodes. Benrekassa locates the novel's meaning in a "space of absent knowledge."

———. "Système métaphorique et pensée politique: Montesquieu et l'imagination mécanique dans *L'Esprit des lois.*" *Revue des Sciences Humaines* 3 (1982): 241–55. Connects Montesquieu's "mechanical curiosity," his interest in technology and machines, to the "mechanical imagination" underlying his political thought that used images like the spring and hydraulics and avoided the organic metaphor.

Bercovici, Daniel. "La Vertu dans les *Lettres persanes*: Significations du mot." *USF Language Quarterly* 16, nos. 1–2 (1977): 53–54, 59. Examines the contexts, associations, and speakers of the term *vertu* to find its multiple shades of meaning.

Betts, C. J. "Some Doubtful Passages in the Text of Montesquieu's *Lettres persanes.*" *Studies on Voltaire and the Eighteenth Century* 230 (1985): 181–88. Proposes a number of corrections for what seem to be lapses in even the "best" editions and manuscripts.

Beyer, Charles. "Montesquieu et le pronom *je* dans *L'Esprit des lois.*" *Cahiers de l'Association Internationale des Etudes Françaises* 35 (1983): 221–34. Traces the different tones and attitudes that Montesquieu adopts: personal, didactic, dialogic, polemic.

Brady, Patrick. "The *Lettres persanes*: Rococo or Neo-Classical?" *Studies on Voltaire and the Eighteenth Century* 53 (1967): 47–77. By analyzing a number of elements (style, characterization, subject, themes, meaning and philosophy, setting, and atmosphere), Brady measures the extent to which this novel is either rococo or neoclassical.

Braun, Theodore. "La Chaîne secrète: A Decade of Interpretations." *French Studies* 42, no. 3 (1988): 278–91. An overview of the most important attempts to explain the "secret chain," concentrating on work done between 1960 and 1973.

Brumfitt, J. H. "Cleopatra's Nose and Enlightenment Historiography." In *Women and Society in Eighteenth-Century France: Essays in Honour of John S. Spink,* edited by Eva Jacobs, 183–94. London: Althone, 1979. Explores the theory of historical causation by which minute causes lead to great events.

Carayol, Elisabeth. "Des lettres persanes oubliées." *Revue d'Histoire Littéraire de la France* 65 (1965): 15–26. The story of eight "persian letters" published in June 1745 in *Fantasque,* a short-lived journal edited in Amsterdam by Saint-Hyacinthe.

Carr, J. L. "The Secret Chain of the *Lettres persanes.*" *Studies on Voltaire and the Eighteenth Century* 55 (1967): 333–44. The secret chain is a political allegory depicting the political situation of Regency France in terms of the harem and its eunuchs.

Carrithers, David W. "Montesquieu, Jefferson, and the Fundamentals of Eighteenth-Century Republican Theory." *French–American Review* 6, no. 2 (Fall 1982): 160–88. Examines Jefferson's "highly selective" reading of the *Laws* between 1774 and 1776 and concludes that Jefferson used Montesquieu as a support and stimulant for his nascent republicanism.

Cherpack, Clifton. "Montesquieu's Usbek: Paper Persian or Anti-Hero?" *Kentucky Romance Quarterly* 18 (1971): 101–10. An unconvincing effort to refute those who see unity (the secret chain) in the novel or any psychological drama in Usbek's internal contradictions.

Cordie, Carlo. "Montesquieu." *Cultura e Scuola* 23, no. 90 (April–June 1984): 74–82. A bibliographical listing with commentary on works on Montesquieu appearing from 1972 to 1980. In Italian.

Crisafulli, Alessandro. "The *Journal des Sçavans* and the *Lettres persanes*." In *Literature and History in the Age of Ideas: Essays on the French Enlightenment Presented to George Havens,* edited by Charles Williams, 59–66. Columbus: Ohio University Press, 1975. Shows that Montesquieu borrowed precise information and anecdotes from the *Journal des Savants* and how he modified that material for his own comic purposes.

Crumpacker, Mary M. "The Secret Chain of the *Lettres persanes* and the Mystery of the B Edition." *Studies on Voltaire and the Eighteenth Century* 102 (1973): 121–41. Argues that the secret chain is not the harem intrigue but Montesquieu's scientific method. Shows that the B or second edition is an earlier draft version that somehow found its way into print.

Dagen, Jean. "La Chaîne des raisons dans les *Lettres persanes*." *Littératures* 17 (Autumn 1987): 71–83. Shows, despite its own obscure style, that the scientific inquiry of the Persians is furthered by the artistic presentation and the technical exploration of the fiction's very nature.

Dauphiné, Claude. "Pourquoi un roman de serail?" *Europe* 574 (1977): 89–96. After a brief review of the traditional criticisms of the oriental intrigue, Dauphiné gives several reasons why it is an integral part of the whole. No single interpretation explored in detail, but a good overview.

Delon, Michel. "Un Monde d'eunuques." *Europe* 574 (1977): 79–88. Eunuchs are men separated from themselves and thus represent an unnatural relation to and exercise of power. They echo certain elements in Usbek and emphasize the situation of women as victims.

Ehrard, Jean. "La Signification politique des *Lettres persanes*." *Archives des Lettres Modernes* 116 (1970): 33–50. Showing the novel's increasingly political content as it progresses, Ehrard argues for a connection between real, historical events and Usbek's political opinions, for example, the parallel between Louis XIV and despotism, the harsh criticism of evil ministers after the Law scandal.

Eskénazi, André. *"Peuple* et *Nation* dans *L'Esprit des loix*: quelques remarques d'un lexicologue."* In *Etudes sur le XVIIIième Siècle,* edited by Jean Ehrard, 41–57. Clermont-Ferrand, France: Association des Publications de la Faculté des Lettres, Université de Clermont II, 1979. Analyzes the semantic fields of these two terms which might seem at first synonymous but which in fact harbor careful distinctions.

Europe 574 (1977). Eleven contributions in this issue are devoted to Montesquieu. Several of particular importance are singled out here.

Fairbairn, A. W. "False Attributions of the *Lettres persanes.*" In *Studies in the French Eighteenth Century Presented to John Lough,* edited by D. J. Mossop, G. E. Rodmell, and D. B. Wilson, 52–65. Durham, England: University of Durham Press, 1978. Examines the speculations in 1721 about the identity of the author of *The Persian Letters* and how Montesquieu delayed admitting his authorship.

Falvey, John. "Aspects of Fictional Creation in the *Lettres persanes,* and of the Aesthetic of the Rationalist Novel." *Romanic Review* 56 (1965): 248–61. Attempts to elaborate a concept of "rational realism" that is different from the conventions of the psychological and sentimental novels and that is based upon Montesquieu's conscious anticipation and manipulation of his reader's reactions.

Fletcher, D. J. "Montesquieu's Concept of Patriotism." *Studies on Voltaire and the Eighteenth Century* 56 (1967): 541–55. Compares Montesquieu's patriotism to that of Rousseau and Voltaire and seeks the influence of England, especially Bolingbroke, and Montesquieu's life as a magistrate.

Forno, Lawrence. "Montesquieu's Reputation in France, England, and America (1755–1800)." *Studies in Burke and His Time* 15 (1973): 5–29. An historical description of how contemporary writers, principally French, reacted to Montesquieu and an evaluation of why they reached these opinions.

Frautschi, Richard. "The Would-Be Invisible Chain in *Les Lettres persanes.*" *French Review* 40 (1967): 604–12. Argues that the chain is "attitudinal" and a "mediating agent" for surprise and astonishment, connecting the digressive philosophical letters and the novelistic sequence.

Gaulin, Michel. "Montesquieu et l'attribution de la lettre XXXIV des *Lettres persanes.*" *Studies on Voltaire and the Eighteenth Century* 79 (1971): 73–78. Proposes several explanations for the change of authorship of this letter from Rica to Usbek in the last two editions.

Gearhart, Suzane. "The Place and Sense of the Outsider: Structuralism in the *Lettres persanes.*" *Modern Language Notes* 92 (1977): 724–48. Using Barthes, Saussure, Lévi-Strauss, and especially Lacan, Gearhart asks if Usbek, as an outsider, represents a critique of Enlightenment ideals based on classical reason and culture.

Gentile, Francesco. "Montesquieu philosophe et sociologue." *Archives des Let-*

tres Modernes 158 (1975): 31–52. An overview of sociologists who recognized Montesquieu as one of themselves and an attempt to locate his "modernity" in his scientific sociology.

Goodman, Dena. "Towards a Critical Vocabulary for Interpretive Fictions of the Eighteenth Century." *Kentucky Romance Quarterly* 31, no. 3 (1984): 259–68. Uses Genette's contrast of description and narration to discuss the challenge to traditional notions of truth in *The Persian Letters.*

Granderoute, Robert. "Montesquieu à travers la presse bordelaise de la deuxième moitié du XVIIIe siècle." *Revue d'Histoire Littéraire de la France* 85 (1985): 1027–43. A summary of how two local journals depicted Montesquieu.

Guyon, Edouard-Félix. "Le Tour d'Europe de Montesquieu 1728–1729." *Revue d'Histoire Diplômatique* 92, nos. 3–4 (1978): 241–61. A summation of Montesquieu's trip through Europe with emphasis on his political and economic observations.

Harari, Josué, and Jane McLelland. "Montesquieu." In *European Writers: The Age of Reason and the Enlightenment,* edited by George Stade and Jane McLelland, 3: 345–66. New York: Scribner's, 1984. An excellent overview that emphasizes the importance of metaphor throughout Montesquieu's work and suggests that the secret chain might be those organic comparisons linking political power, the body politic, and the despotic harem.

Harris, Micheline F. "Le Séjour de Montesquieu en Italie (août 1728–juillet 1729): Chronologie et commentaires." *Studies on Voltaire and the Eighteenth Century* 127 (1974): 65–197. Supplementing the *Voyage* with additional information culled from the correspondence, Harris reconstructs sometimes a daily calendar of events during Montesquieu's stay in Italy.

Hopp, Lajos. "*Lettres persanes* et *Lettres de Turquie.*" *French Studies* 21 (1967): 220–28. Seeks the possible influences of Montesquieu on the eighteenth-century Hungarian author Kelemen Mikes.

Kempf, Roger. "*Les Lettres persanes* ou le corps absent." *Tel Quel* 22 (1965): 81–86. A short but provocative analysis on separation and absence: eunuchs separated from themselves, the voyage as a separation/castration, and Usbek's own physical fatigue and absence from his wives.

Kra, Pauline. "The Invisible Chain in the *Lettres persanes.*" *Studies on Voltaire and the Eighteenth Century* 23 (1963): 7–60. Argues that the secret chain is the grouping of letters by topic. Full meaning is produced by context and the interrelationships of themes and letters.

———. "Montesquieu and Women." In *French Women and the Age of Enlightenment,* edited by Samia Spencer, 272–84. Bloomington: Indiana University Press, 1984. Synthesizes Montesquieu's thinking about women, including a reconstruction of views presented in his fiction, and finds him an intelligent defender of women's rights.

————. "The Role of the Harem in Imitations of Montesquieu's *Lettres per-sanes.*" *Studies on Voltaire and the Eighteenth Century* 182 (1979): 273–83. Citing the *Lettres persanes* and three imitations, Kra illustrates the meta-phorical function of the harem which was used to demonstrate the inferior status of women or an equivalent of the convent.

Larrère, Catherine. "Les Typologies des gouvernements chez Montesquieu." In *Etudes sur le XVIIIe Siècle,* edited by Jean Ehrard, 87–103. Clemont-Ferrand, France: Association des Publications de la Faculté des Lettres, Université de Clermont II, 1979. Studies the opposition and eventual resolution of two typologies: one, more sociological, is the familiar tri-partite distinction of monarchy, republic, and despotism; the other, more political, is the binary distinction between extreme and moderate.

Laufer, Roger. "La Réussite romanesque et la signification des *Lettres persanes* de Montesquieu." *Revue d'Histoire Littéraire de la France* 61 (1961): 188–203. This groundbreaking essay argued that the oriental intrigue was an essential part of the whole book and that it constituted the secret chain that gave it unity.

Leigh, R. A. "Le Thème de la justice dans les *Lettres persanes.*" *Cahiers de l'Association Internationale des Etudes Françaises* 35 (1983): 201–19. Justice is the sole absolute value, the unique inspiration for human behavior when seen against the moral and social anarchy of the Regency.

Magné, Bernard. "Une Source de la 'Lettre persane' XXXVIII? *L'Egalité des deux sexes* de Poullain de la Barre." *Revue d'Histoire Littéraire de la France* 68 (1968): 407–14. Refutes the identification of Fontenelle as the *galant philosophe* in this letter and proposes La Barre as this defender of women's rights and proponent of her equality with men.

Mason, Sheila. "An Essentialist Inheritance: From Hooker to Montesquieu." *Studies on Voltaire and the Eighteenth Century* 242 (1986): 83–124. Exam-ines Montesquieu's debt to thinkers like Malbranche, Bayle, and espe-cially Hooker on natural law, morality, and the nature of justice.

————. "The Riddle of Roxane." In *Women and Society in Eighteenth-Century France: Essays in Honour of John S. Spink,* edited by Eva Jacobs, 28–41. London: Althone, 1979. Discusses apparent contradictions of his views on women's political rights and their place in marriage. Concludes that he is neither—or both—misogynist or feminist.

Mass, Edgar. "Le Développement textuel et les lectures contemporaines des *Lettres persanes.*" *Cahiers de l'Association Internationale des Etudes Françaises* 35 (1983): 185–200. Close textual analysis of the various editions.

McLelland, Jane. "Metaphor in Montesquieu's Theoretical Writings." *Studies on Voltaire and the Eighteenth Century* 199 (1981): 205–24. Sees Montes-quieu's use of metaphor as a connection between his scientific interests and his political thinking. Comparison is a way of knowing.

Mercier, Roger. "Le Roman dans les *Lettres persanes*: Structure et signification." *Revue des Sciences Humaines* 107 (July–September 1962): 345–56. Describes how the harem intrigue complements the philosophical and political ideas about happiness, virtue, and liberty. The fiction frees the didactic elements of rigidity.

Milhaud, Gérard. "Le Regard scientifique de Montesquieu." *Europe* 574 (1977): 31–41. This analysis of Montesquieu's scientific method concludes that, despite his gift for and interest in science, he was a "poor observer and an imprudent experimenter."

Newmark, Kevin. "Leaving Home without It." *Stanford French Review* 11, no. 1 (Spring 1987): 17–32. Travel and translation are seen here as violent twins. Imaginative, emotional reading is a violence done to reason, just as Usbek the master perpetrates violence on his slaves and as translation does violence to meaning.

O'Reilly, Robert. "Montesquieu: Anti-feminist." *Studies on Voltaire and the Eighteenth Century* 102 (1973): 143–56. Argues that Montesquieu's masculine prejudices overwhelmed his reason when he discussed natural law and woman's role in the state.

———. "The Structure and Meaning of the *Lettres persanes.*" *Studies on Voltaire and the Eighteenth Century* 67 (1969): 91–131. A fine traditional analysis of the literary aspects and techniques of the novel. Argues that the secret chain is "the ironic point of view of an implied author" who illustrates the "*décalage* between Usbek's ideas and his actions."

Pascal, Jean-Noel. "Montesquieu romancier après les *Lettres persanes*: Note sur *Arsace et Ismenie,* histoire orientale." *Littératures* 17 (Autumn 1987): 85–91. Attempts to "rediscover" this minor oriental tale by accenting the political and ideological themes it shares with other works.

Picard, Bernard. "La Pensée et l'action dans les *Lettres persanes.*" *French Review* 42 (1969): 857–64. The contradiction between Usbek's philosophical thinking in France and his despotic actions in Persia puts the efficacy of reason in doubt and underlines the need to seek liberty in conformity with the laws of nature.

Raymond, Agnès. "Encore quelques réflexions sur la 'chaîne secrète' des *Lettres persanes.*" *Studies on Voltaire and the Eighteenth Century* 89 (1972): 1337–47. While the image of the chain is a commonplace in philosophic language, for Montesquieu it connects religion, woman's condition, despotism, and John Law's system.

Roddick, Nick. "The Structure of the *Lettres persanes.*" *French Studies* 28 (1974): 396–407. The secret chain is the intercalation of Persian elements through the first two-thirds of the novel. In the last third, the Persian elements are gathered together even though their dates suggest the same sprinkling distribution as before.

Singerman, Alan J. "Réflexions sur une métaphore: Le sérail dans les *Lettres persanes.*" *Studies on Voltaire and the Eighteenth Century* 185 (1980): 181–98. Sees the symbolic role of eunuchs integrated into the whole novel: eunuchs are ministers and courtesans; they wield power they should not have; and they emphasize the separation of Usbek the thinker from any practical action.

Spruell, Shelby O. "The Metaphorical Use of Sexual Repression to Represent Political Oppression in Montesquieu's *Persian Letters*." *Proceedings of the Annual Meeting of the Western Society for French History* 8 (1981): 147–58. A good analysis of an "explosive" and "subversive" issue: sexuality as an image of the struggle for liberty, eroticism as a mask for the will to power. Roxane's desire for self-determination is locked in mortal combat with the authoritarian power of Usbek.

Starobinski, Jean. "*Les Lettres persanes*: Apparence et essence." *Neohelicon*, 2, nos. 1–2 (1974): 83–112. A provocative analysis of many overlooked details like the fiction of the author as editor and the refusal to name any Frenchmen. This essay also serves as the preface to the Folio edition of the novel.

Strong, Susan C. "Why a Secret Chain? Oriental Topoi and the Essential Mystery of the *Lettres persanes*." *Studies on Voltaire and the Eighteenth Century* 230 (1985): 167–79. Finds the secret chain in the eighteenth-century reader's emotional involvement in Usbek's dilemma, the schizoid split between his public and private behaviors.

Testud, Pierre. "Les *Lettres persanes*, roman épistolaire." *Revue d'Histoire Littéraire de la France* 66 (October–December 1966): 642–56. An intelligent exploration of the effects of the epistolary format: multiple viewpoints, the intimacy of various "I's," dialogue among correspondents, a theatrical present tense, and numerous "absences."

Thomas, Ruth. "Montesquieu's Harem and Diderot's Convent: The Woman as Prisoner." *French Review* 52 (1978): 36–45. An intelligent comparison of these two female institutions and their "denaturalizing and desocializing effects."

Todorov, Tzvetan. "Droit naturel et formes de gouvernement dans *L'Esprit des lois*." *Esprit* 75 (March 1983): 35–48. Reorganizing Montesquieu in his own schemas, Todorov articulates his own unifying structure for the *Laws*, in which he sees moderation as the keystone, legality as the bulwark of liberty, and despotism as any unshared use of power.

———. "Réflexions sur les *Lettres persanes*." *Romanic Review* 74, no. 3 (May 1983): 306–15. Asking questions rather than giving straight answers, Todorov focuses on three points: the limits of the outsider's ability to see, be he Usbek, Montesquieu, or the reader; relativism that leads to absolutes; and the dilemma of force versus reason and how the latter can so easily lose to the former.

Trumpener, Katie. "Rewriting Roxane: Orientalism and Intertextuality in Montesquieu's *Lettres persanes* and Defoe's *The Fortunate Mistress*." *Stanford French Review* 11, no. 2 (Summer 1987): 177–91. Reads Racine, Montesquieu, and DeFoe each in the light of the others and thus evokes the intertextuality of woman as slave, sexually desirable and yet unattainable.

Van Den Abbeele, Georges. "Montesquieu *touriste,* or a View from the Top." *L'Esprit Créateur* 25, no. 3 (Fall 1985): 64–74. While prone to some dubious puns, the author sees the "vertical view" from the tower as an emblem of Montesquieu the tourist seeing sights and the theorist seeking an all-encompassing vision of his subject matter.

Vartanian, Aram. "Eroticism and Politics in the *Lettres persanes.*" *Romanic Review* 60 (1969): 23–33. The seraglio is not the "sauce" but the "substance" of this novel's philosophical food. It teaches the same lesson as the Troglodytes but from the opposite side and on the affective level. Eroticism reflects the most basic, biological need for human freedom.

Viselli, Sante, and Alexandre Amprimoz. "Voyage et esprit chez Montesquieu." *USF Language Quarterly* 25, nos. 1–2 (Fall–Winter 1986): 47–49, 53. Confusing critical notions and vocabulary and making him a precursor of Baudelaire, the authors try to describe the real and symbolic values of Montesquieu's actual and imaginary (i.e., through reading) voyages.

Wardman, H. W. "*Les Lettres persanes.*" *Essays in French Literature* (Western Australia) 3 (1966): 65–77. While not conceding that *The Persian Letters* is a novel, Wardman does see it as a fiction that "portrays reality as fictional or as imbued with the imaginary."

Weil, Françoise. "Voyages et curiosités politiques avant l'*Encyclopédie*: Le Voyage en Italie de Montesquieu et de Brosses." In *Modèles et Moyens de la réflexion politique au XVIIIe Siècle,* edited by Jacques Decobert, 1: 153–73. Lille, France: Publications de l'Université de Lille III, 1977. Compares a sample of travelers and what they wrote, with emphasis on Montesquieu and de Brosses. Finds them the most intelligent and observant, curious about the social, commercial, and political realities of the countries they visited.

Index

The Author

Peter V. Conroy, Jr., is professor of French at the University of Illinois, Chicago, where he has served two terms as chairman of the department. In June 1990 Professor Conroy was awarded the *Prix d'Excellence* by the Chicago/Northern Illinois chapter of the American Association of Teachers of French in recognition of his teaching and his scholarship. He is the author of *Techniques of the Novel,* a monograph on the novelist Crébillion fils, and of *Intimate, Intrusive, and Triumphant: Readers in the "Liaisons dangereuses,"* a study of Choderlos de Laclos. He has written more than 30 articles on a variety of eighteenth-century topics and on such individual authors as Molière, Scarron, Zola, Proust, and Camus.

The Editor

David O'Connell is professor of foreign languages and chair of the Department of Foreign Languages at Georgia State University. He received his Ph.D. from Princeton University in 1966, where he was a National Woodrow Wilson Fellow, the Bergen Fellow in Romance Languages, and a National Woodrow Wilson Dissertation Fellow. He is the author of *The Teachings of Saint Louis: A Critical Text* (1972), *Les Propos de Saint Louis* (1974), *Louis-Ferdinand Céline* (1976), *The Instructions of Saint Louis: A Critical Text* (1979), and *Michel de Saint Pierre: A Catholic Novelist at the Crossroads* (1990). He is the editor of *Catholic Writers in France since 1945* (1983) and has served as review editor (1977–79) and managing editor (1987–90) of the *French Review*.